1

Printed in the United States of America

ParaPro Essential Test Tips DVD
from Trivium Test Prep!

Dear Customer,

Thank you for purchasing from Trivium Test Prep! We're honored to help you prepare for your ParaPro.

To show our appreciation, we're offering a **FREE *ParaPro Essential Test Tips* DVD by Trivium Test Prep**. Our DVD includes 35 test preparation strategies that will make you successful on the ParaPro. All we ask is that you email us your feedback and describe your experience with our product. Amazing, awful, or just so-so: we want to hear what you have to say!

To receive your **FREE *ParaPro Essential Test Tips* DVD**, please email us at 5star@triviumtestprep.com. Include "Free 5 Star" in the subject line and the following information in your email:

1. The title of the product you purchased.
2. Your rating from 1 – 5 (with 5 being the best).
3. Your feedback about the product, including how our materials helped you meet your goals and ways in which we can improve our products.
4. Your full name and shipping address so we can send your FREE *ParaPro Essential Test Tips* DVD.

If you have any questions or concerns please feel free to contact us directly at 5star@triviumtestprep.com.

Thank you!

- Trivium Test Prep Team

Table of Contents

Introduction

The fact that you've purchased this book means two things. The first: You're preparing for, or at least considering, the ParaPro exam. The second: You've already made an excellent first step in picking up this study guide.

We'll provide you with a detailed overview of the ParaPro, so that you know exactly what to expect on test day. We'll also cover all of the subjects over which you will be tested, as well as provide multiple practice sections for you to test your knowledge and improve. No worries – even if it's been a while since your last major examination, we'll make sure you're more than ready!

What is the ParaPro?

The ParaPro exam developed by ETS to measure the skills of reading, writing, and math for prospective and practicing paraprofessionals in response to the federal legislation known as the No Child Left Behind Act. Along with holding an associates of the arts degree (or 2 years of college courses completed), passing the ParaPro Assessment is a requirement for anyone wanting to instruct children in the classroom.

Breaking Down the ParaPro Assesment Exam

You will have 2.5 hours to complete all sections of the test of which there are a total of 90 questions. Those sections are:

- **Writing**
  - o 30 Questions: Tests knowledge of vocabulary, grammar and usage.

- **Math**
  - o 30 Questions: Tests knowledge of math (pre-algebra, algebra, geometry, etc.)

- **Reading**
  - o 30 Questions: Tests reading comprehension through questions over multiple passages.

Scoring

The makers of the test do not set a qualifying or passing score. Instead, each state or district sets their own requirements for minimum standards, so it is important to check with the school district of where you plan to teach.

How This Book Works

The subsequent chapters in this book are divided into a review of those topics covered on the exam. This is not to "teach" or "re-teach" you these concepts – there is no way to cram all of that material into one book! Instead, we are going to help you recall all of the information which you've already learned. Even more importantly, we'll show you how to apply that knowledge.

Each chapter includes an extensive review, with practice drills at the end to test your knowledge. With time, practice, and determination, you'll be well-prepared for test day.

Chapter 1: Reading

The ParaPro reading section consists of several multiple-choice questions, which will measure your ability to understand, analyze, and evaluate written passages. The passages will contain material from a variety of sources, and will cover a number of different topics.

Questions for each passage will call for knowledge of the following:

1. Specific details and facts.
2. Comparisons and analogies.
3. Inferences.
4. Word meaning through context.
5. Main idea of sections or the passage as a whole.
6. Author's tone and/or point of view.

At the end of this chapter, we will have a "Test Your Knowledge" section, which will give you an opportunity to practice reading a passage and answering questions – just as you will on the ParaPro. While a good vocabulary can help, the only way to get better at the reading section is to practice, practice, practice. It is, however, vitally important that you practice the way you want to perform on test day. Form good habits now by actively reading and making notes.

But first, let's freshen up on our reading comprehension skills.

The Main Idea

The main idea of a text is the purpose behind why a writer would choose to write a book, article, story, etc. Being able to find and understand the main idea is a critical skill necessary to comprehend and appreciate what you're reading.

Consider a political election. A candidate is running for office and plans to deliver a speech asserting her position on tax reform. The **topic** of the speech—tax reform—is clear to voters, and probably of interest to many. However, imagine that the candidate believes that taxes should be lowered. She is likely to assert this argument in her speech, supporting it with examples proving why lowering taxes would benefit the public and how it could be accomplished. While the topic of the speech would be tax reform, the benefit of lowering taxes would be the **main idea**. Other candidates may have different perspectives on the topic; they may believe that higher taxes are necessary, or that current taxes are adequate. It is likely that their speeches, while on the same topic of tax reform, would have different main ideas: different arguments likewise supported by different examples. Determining what a speaker, writer, or text is asserting about a specific issue will reveal the main idea.

One more quick note: the exam may also ask about a passage's **theme**, which is similar to but distinct from its topic. While a topic is usually a specific *person, place, thing,* or *issue,* the theme is an *idea* or *concept* that the author refers back to frequently. Examples of common themes include ideas like the importance of family, the dangers of technology, and the beauty of nature.

There will be many questions on the exam that require you to differentiate between the topic, theme, and main idea of a passage. Let's look at an example passage to see how you would answer these questions.

"Babe Didrikson Zaharias, one of the most decorated female athletes of the twentieth century, is an inspiration for everyone. Born in 1911 in Beaumont, Texas, Zaharias lived in a time when women were

7

considered second-class to men, but she never let that stop her from becoming a champion. Babe was one of seven children in a poor immigrant family, and was competitive from an early age. As a child she excelled at most things she tried, especially sports, which continued into high school and beyond. After high school, Babe played amateur basketball for two years, and soon after began training in track and field. Despite the fact that women were only allowed to enter in three events, Babe represented the United States in the 1932 Los Angeles Olympics, and won two gold medals and one silver for track and field events.

"In the early 1930s, Babe began playing golf which earned her a legacy. The first tournament she entered was a men's only tournament, however she did not make the cut to play. Playing golf as an amateur was the only option for a woman at this time, since there was no professional women's league. Babe played as an amateur for a little over a decade, until she turned pro in 1947 for the Ladies Professional Golf Association (LPGA) of which she was a founding member. During her career as a golfer, Babe won eighty-two tournaments, amateur and professional, including the U.S. Women's Open, All-American Open, and British Women's Open Golf Tournament. In 1953, Babe was diagnosed with cancer, but fourteen weeks later, she played in a tournament. That year she won her third U.S. Women's Open. However by 1955, she didn't have the physicality to compete anymore, and she died of the disease in 1956."

The topic of this paragraph is obviously Babe Zaharias—the whole passage describes events from her life. Determining the main idea, however, requires a little more analysis. The passage describes Babe Zaharias' life, but the main idea of the paragraph is what it says *about* her life. To figure out the main idea, consider what the writer is saying about Babe Zaharias. The writer is saying that she's someone to admire—that's the main idea and what unites all the information in the paragraph. Lastly, what might the theme of the passage be? The writer refers to several broad concepts, including never giving up and overcoming the odds, both of which could be themes for the passage. Two major indicators of the main idea of a paragraph or passage follow below:

- It is a general idea; it applies to all the more specific ideas in the passage. Every other sentence in a paragraph should be able to relate in some way to the main idea.
- It asserts a specific viewpoint that the author supports with facts, opinions, or other details. In other words, the main idea takes a stand.

Example
From so far away it's easy to imagine the surface of our solar system's planets as enigmas—how could we ever know what those far-flung planets really look like? It turns out, however, that scientists have a number of tools at their disposal that allow them to paint detailed pictures of many planets' surfaces. The topography of Venus, for example, has been explored by several space probes, including the Russian Venera landers and NASA's Magellan orbiter. These craft used imaging and radar to map the surface of the planet, identifying a whole host of features including volcanoes, craters, and a complex system of channels. Mars has similarly been mapped by space probes, including the famous Mars Rovers, which are automated vehicles that actually landed on the surface of Mars. These rovers have been used by NASA and other space agencies to study the geology, climate, and possible biology of the planet.

In addition these long-range probes, NASA has also used its series of orbiting telescopes to study distant planets. These four massively powerful telescopes include the famous Hubble Space Telescope as well as the Compton Gamma Ray Observatory, Chandra X-Ray Observatory, and the Spitzer Space Telescope. Scientists can use these telescopes to examine planets using not only visible light but also infrared and near-infrared light, ultraviolet light, x-rays and gamma rays.

Powerful telescopes aren't just found in space: NASA makes use of Earth-bound telescopes as well. Scientists at the National Radio Astronomy Observatory in Charlottesville, VA, have spent decades using radio imaging to build an incredibly detailed portrait of Venus' surface. In fact, Earth-bound telescopes offer a distinct advantage over orbiting telescopes because they allow scientists to capture data from a fixed point, which in turn allows them to effectively compare data collected over long period of time.

Which of the following sentences best describes the main of the passage?

A)   It's impossible to know what the surfaces of other planets are really like.
B)   Telescopes are an important tool for scientists studying planets in our solar system.
C)   Venus' surface has many of the same features as the Earth's, including volcanoes, craters, and channels.
D)   Scientists use a variety of advanced technologies to study the surface of the planets in our solar system.

Answer: Answer A) can be eliminated because it directly contradicts the rest of the passage, which goes into detail about how scientists have learned about the surfaces of other planets. Answers B) and C) can also be eliminated because they offer only specific details from the passage—while both choices contain details from the passage, neither is general enough to encompass the passage as a whole. Only answer D) provides an assertion that is both backed up by the passage's content and general enough to cover the entire passage.

Topic and Summary Sentences
The main idea of a paragraph usually appears within the topic sentence. The **topic sentence** introduces the main idea to readers; it indicates not only the topic of a passage, but also the writer's perspective on the topic. Notice, for example, how the first sentence in the example paragraph about Babe Zaharias states the main idea: *Babe Didrikson Zaharias, one of the most decorated female athletes of the twentieth century, is an inspiration for everyone.*
Even though paragraphs generally begin with topic sentences due to their introductory nature, on occasion writers build up to the topic sentence by using supporting details in order to generate interest or build an argument. Be alert for paragraphs when writers do not include a clear topic sentence at all; even without a clear topic sentence, a paragraph will still have a main idea. You may also see a **summary sentence** at the end of a passage. As its name suggests, this sentence sums up the passage, often by restating the main idea and the author's key evidence supporting it.

Example
In the following paragraph, what are the topic and summary sentences?

The Constitution of the United States establishes a series of limits to rein in centralized power. Separation of powers distributes federal authority among three competing branches: the executive, the legislative, and the judicial. Checks and balances allow the branches to check the usurpation of power by any one branch. States' rights are protected under the Constitution from too much encroachment by the federal government. Enumeration of powers names the specific and few powers the federal government has. These four restrictions have helped sustain the American republic for over two centuries.

Answer: The topic sentence is the first sentence in the paragraph. It introduces the topic of discussion, in this case the constitutional limits aimed at resisting centralized power. The summary sentence is the last sentence in the paragraph. It sums up the information that was just presented: here, that constitutional limits have helped sustain the United States of America for over two hundred years.

Implied Main Idea

A paragraph without a clear topic sentence still has a main idea; rather than clearly stated, it is implied. Determining the **implied main idea** requires some detective work: you will need to look at the author's word choice and tone in addition to the content of the passage to find his or her main idea. Let's look at an example paragraph.

Example

One of my summer reading books was Mockingjay. *Though it's several hundred pages long, I read it in just a few days. I was captivated by the adventures of the main character and the complicated plot of the book. However, I felt like the ending didn't reflect the excitement of the story. Given what a powerful personality the main character has, I felt like the ending didn't do her justice.*

Even without a clear topic sentence, this paragraph has a main idea. What is the writer's perspective on the book—what is the writer saying about it?

A) *Mockingjay* is a terrific novel.
B) *Mockingjay* is disappointing.
C) *Mockingjay* is full of suspense.
D) *Mockingjay* is a lousy novel.

The correct answer is B): the novel is disappointing. The process of elimination will reveal the correct answer if that is not immediately clear. While that the paragraph begins with positive commentary on the book—*I was captivated by the adventures of the main character and the complicated plot of the book*—this positive idea is followed by the contradictory transition word *however*. A) cannot be the correct answer because the author concludes that the novel was poor. Likewise, D) cannot be correct because it does not encompass all the ideas in the paragraph; despite the negative conclusion, the author enjoyed most of the book. The main idea should be able to encompass all of the thoughts in a paragraph; choice D) does not apply to the beginning of this paragraph. Finally, choice C) is too specific; it could only apply to the brief description of the plot and adventures of the main character. That leaves choice B) as the best option. The author initially enjoyed the book, but was disappointed by the ending, which seemed unworthy of the exciting plot and character.

Fortunately, none of Alyssa's coworkers has ever seen inside the large filing drawer in her desk. Disguised by the meticulous neatness of the rest of her workspace, there was no sign of the chaos beneath. To even open it, she had to struggle for several minutes with the enormous pile of junk jamming the drawer, until it would suddenly give way, and papers, folders, and candy wrappers spilled out of the top and onto the floor. It was an organizational nightmare, with torn notes and spreadsheets haphazardly thrown on top of each other, and melted candy smeared across pages. She was worried the odor would soon permeate to her coworker's desks, revealing to them her secret.

Which sentence best describes the main idea of the paragraph above?

A) Alyssa wishes she could move to a new desk.
B) Alyssa wishes she had her own office.
C) Alyssa is glad none of her coworkers know about her messy drawer.
D) Alyssa is sad because she doesn't have any coworkers.

Clearly, Alyssa has a messy drawer, and C) is the right answer. The paragraph begins by indicating her gratitude that her coworkers do not know about her drawer (*Fortunately, none of Alyssa's coworkers has ever seen inside the large filing drawer in her desk.*) Plus, notice how the drawer is described: *it was an organizational nightmare*, and it apparently doesn't even function properly: *to even open the drawer, she had to struggle for several minutes.* The writer reveals that it has an odor, with *melted candy* inside. Alyssa is clearly ashamed of her drawer and fearful of being judged by her coworkers for it.

Specific Details and Facts

Specific details and facts provide more support for the author's main idea. For instance, in the Babe Zaharias example above, the writer makes the general assertion that *Babe Didrikson Zaharias, one of the most decorated female athletes of the twentieth century, is an inspiration for everyone.* The other sentences offer specific facts and details that prove why Babe Zaharias is an inspiration: the struggles she faced as a female athlete, and the specific years she competed in the Olympics and in golf.

Writers often provide clues that can help you identify supporting details. These **signal words** tell you that a supporting fact or idea will follow, and so can be helpful in identifying supporting details. Signal words can also help you rule out sentences that are not the main idea or topic sentence: if a sentence begins with one of these phrases, it will likely be too specific to be a main idea.

Questions on the ParaPro will ask you to do two things with supporting details: you will need to find details that support a particular idea and also explain why a particular detail was included in the passage. In order to answer these questions, you need to have a solid understanding of the passage's main idea. With this knowledge, you can determine how a supporting detail fits in with the larger structure of the passage.

Example

From so far away it's easy to imagine the surface of our solar system's planets as enigmas—how could we ever know what those far-flung planets really look like? It turns out, however, that scientists have a number of tools at their disposal that allow them to paint detailed pictures of many planets' surfaces. The topography of Venus, for example, has been explored by several space probes, including the Russian *Venera* landers and NASA's *Magellan* orbiter. These craft used imaging and radar to map the surface of the planet, identifying a whole host of features including volcanoes, craters, and a complex system of channels. Mars has similarly been mapped by space probes, including the famous Mars Rovers, which are automated vehicles that actually landed on the surface of Mars. These rovers have been used by NASA and other space agencies to study the geology, climate, and possible biology of the planet.

In addition these long-range probes, NASA has also used its series of orbiting telescopes to study distant planets. These four massively powerful telescopes include the famous Hubble Space Telescope as well as the Compton Gamma Ray Observatory, Chandra X-Ray Observatory, and the Spitzer Space Telescope. Scientists can use these telescopes to examine planets using not only visible light but also infrared and near-infrared light, ultraviolet light, x-rays and gamma rays.

Powerful telescopes aren't just found in space: NASA makes use of Earth-bound telescopes as well. Scientists at the National Radio Astronomy Observatory in Charlottesville, VA, have spent decades using radio imaging to build an incredibly detailed portrait of Venus' surface. In fact, Earth-bound telescopes offer a distinct advantage over orbiting telescopes because they allow scientists to capture data from a fixed point, which in turn allows them to effectively compare data collected over long period of time.

Which sentence from the text best helps develop the idea that scientists make use of many different technologies to study the surfaces of other planets?

A)   These rovers have been used by NASA and other space agencies to study the geology, climate, and possible biology of the planet.

B)   From so far away it's easy to imagine the surface of our solar system's planets as enigmas—how could we ever know what those far-flung planets really look like?

C)   In addition these long-range probes, NASA has also used its series of orbiting telescopes to study distant planets.

D)   These craft used imaging and radar to map the surface of the planet, identifying a whole host of features including volcanoes, craters, and a complex system of channels.

Answer: You're looking for detail from the passage that supports the main idea—scientists make use of many different technologies to study the surfaces of other planets. Answer A) includes a specific detail about rovers, but does not offer any details that support the idea of multiple technologies being used. Similarly, answer D) provides another specific detail about space probes. Answer B) doesn't provide any supporting details; it simply introduces the topic of the passage. Only answer C) provides a detail that directly supports the author's assertion that scientists use multiple technologies to study the planets.

If true, which detail could be added to the passage above to support the author's argument that scientists use many different technologies to study the surface of planets?

A)   Because the Earth's atmosphere blocks x-rays, gamma rays, and infrared radiation, NASA needed to put telescopes in orbit above the atmosphere.

B)   In 2015, NASA released a map of Venus which was created by compiling images from orbiting telescopes and long-range space probes.

C)   NASA is currently using the *Curiosity* and *Opportunity* rovers to look for signs of ancient life on Mars.

D)   NASA has spent over $2.5 billion to build, launch, and repair the Hubble Space Telescope.

Answer: You can eliminate answers C) and D) because they don't address the topic of studying the surface of planets. Answer A) can also be eliminated because it only addresses a single technology. Only choice B) provides would add support to the author's claim about the importance of using multiple technologies.

The author likely included the detail *Earth-bound telescopes offer a distinct advantage over orbiting telescopes because they allow scientists to capture data from a fixed point* in order to:

A)   Explain why it has taken scientists so long to map the surface of Venus.

B)   Suggest that Earth-bound telescopes are the most important equipment used by NASA scientists.

C)   Prove that orbiting telescopes will soon be replaced by Earth-bound telescopes.

D)   Demonstrate why NASA scientists rely on my different types of scientific equipment.

Answer: Only answer D) directs directly to the author's main argument. The author doesn't mention how long it has taken to map the surface of Venus (answer A), nor does he say that one technology is more important than the others (answer B). And while this detail does highlight the advantages of using Earth-bound telescopes, the author's argument is that many technologies are being used at the same time, so there's no reason to think that orbiting telescopes will be replaced (answer C).

Facts vs. Opinions

On the exam Reading passages you might be asked to identify a statement in a passage as either a fact or an opinion, so you'll need to know the difference between the two. A **fact** is a statement or thought that can be proven to be true. The statement *Wednesday comes after Tuesday* is a fact—you can point to a calendar to prove it. In contrast, an **opinion** is an assumption that is not based in fact and cannot be proven to be true. The assertion that *television is more entertaining than feature films* is an opinion—people will disagree on this, and there's no reference you can use to prove or disprove it.

Example

Exercise is critical for healthy development in children. Today, there is an epidemic of unhealthy children in the United States who will face health problems in adulthood due to poor diet and lack of exercise as children. This is a problem for all Americans, especially with the rising cost of healthcare.
It is vital that school systems and parents encourage their children to engage in a minimum of thirty minutes of cardiovascular exercise each day, mildly increasing their heart rate for a sustained period. This is proven to decrease the likelihood of developmental diabetes, obesity, and a multitude of other health problems. Also, children need a proper diet rich in fruits and vegetables so that they can grow and develop physically, as well as learn healthy eating habits early on.

> Which of the following is a fact in the passage, not an opinion?
> A)   Fruits and vegetables are the best way to help children be healthy.
> B)   Children today are lazier than they were in previous generations.
> C)   The risk of diabetes in children is reduced by physical activity.
> D)   Children should engage in thirty minutes of exercise a day.

Answer: Choice B) can be discarded immediately because it is negative and is not discussed anywhere in the passage. Answers A) and D) are both opinions—the author is promoting exercise, fruits, and vegetables as a way to make children healthy. (Notice that these incorrect answers contain words that hint at being an opinion such as *best*, *should*, or other comparisons.) Answer B), on the other hand, is a simple fact stated by the author; it's introduced by the word *proven* to indicate that you don't need to just take the author's word for it.

The Author's Purpose and Tone

Whenever an author writes a text, she always has a purpose, whether that's to entertain, inform, explain, or persuade. A short story, for example, is meant to entertain, while an online news article would be designed to inform the public about a current event.

Each of these different types of writing has a specific name. On the exam, you may be asked to identify which of these categories a passage fits into:

- **Narrative writing** tells a story. (novel, short story, play)
- **Expository writing** informs people. (newspaper and magazine articles)
- **Technical writing** explains something. (product manual, directions)
- **Persuasive writing** tries to convince the reader of something. (opinion column on a blog)

You may also be asked about primary and secondary sources. These terms describe not the writing itself but the author's relationship to what's being written about. A **primary source** is an unaltered piece of writing that was composed during the time when the events being described took place; these texts are often written by the people involved. A **secondary source** might address the same topic but provides extra commentary or analysis. These texts can be written by people not directly involved in the events. For example, a book written by a political candidate to inform people about his or her stand on an issue is a primary source; an online article written by a journalist analyzing how that position will affect the election is a secondary source.

Example

Elizabeth closed her eyes and braced herself on the armrests that divided her from her fellow passengers. Take-off was always the worst part for her. The revving of the engines, the way her stomach dropped as the plane lurched upward: it made her feel sick. Then, she had to watch the world fade away beneath her, getting smaller and smaller until it was just her and the clouds hurtling through the sky. Sometimes (but only sometimes) it just had to be endured, though. She focused on the thought of her sister's smiling face and her new baby nephew as the plane slowly pulled onto the runway.

The passage above is reflective of which type of writing?
A)   Narrative
B)   Expository
C)   Technical
D)   Persuasive

Answer: The passage is telling a story—we meet Elizabeth and learn about her fear of flying—so it's a narrative text. There is no factual information presented or explained, nor is the author trying to persuade the reader.

Inferences and Drawing Conclusions

In addition to understanding the main idea and factual content of a passage, you'll also be asked to take your analysis one step further and anticipate what other information could logically be added to the passage. In a non-fiction passage, for example, you might be asked which statement the author of the passage would agree with. In an excerpt from a fictional work, you might be asked to anticipate what the character would do next.

To answer these questions, you need to have a solid understanding of the topic, theme, and main idea of the passage; armed with this information, you can figure out which of the answer choices best fits within those criteria (or alternatively, which ones do not). For example, if the author of the passage is advocating for safer working conditions in textile factories, any supporting details that would be added to the passage should support that idea. You might add sentences that contain information about the number of accidents that occur in textile factories or that outline a new plan for fire safety.

Example

Today, there is an epidemic of unhealthy children in the United States who will face health problems in adulthood due to poor diet and lack of exercise during their childhood. This is a problem for all Americans, as adults with chronic health issues are adding to the rising cost of healthcare. A child who grows up living an unhealthy lifestyle is likely to become an adult who does the same.

Because exercise is critical for healthy development in children, it is vital that school systems and parents encourage their children to engage in a minimum of thirty minutes of cardiovascular exercise each day. Even this small amount of exercise has been proven to decrease the likelihood that young people will develop diabetes, obesity, and other health issues as adults. In addition to exercise, children need a proper diet rich in fruits and vegetables so that they can grow and develop physically. Starting a good diet early also teaches children healthy eating habits they will carry into adulthood.

The author of this passage would most likely agree with which statement?

A)   Parents are solely responsible for the health of their children.

B)   Children who do not want to exercise should not be made to.

C)   Improved childhood nutrition will help lower the amount Americans spend on healthcare.

D)   It's not important to teach children healthy eating habits because they will learn them as adults.

Answer: The author would most likely support answer C): he mentions in the first paragraph that unhealthy habits are adding to the rising cost of healthcare. The main idea of the passage is that nutrition and exercise are important for children, so answer B) doesn't make sense—the author would likely support measures to encourage children to exercise. Answers A) and D) can also be eliminated because they are directly contradicted in the text. The author specifically mentions the role of schools systems, so he doesn't believe parents are solely responsible for their children's health. He also specifically states that children who grow up with unhealthy habit will become adults with unhealthy habits, which contradicts D).

Elizabeth closed her eyes and braced herself on the armrests that divided her from her fellow passengers. Take-off was always the worst part for her. The revving of the engines, the way her stomach dropped as the plane lurched upward: it made her feel sick. Then, she had to watch the world fade away beneath her, getting smaller and smaller until it was just her and the clouds hurtling through the sky. Sometimes (but only sometimes) it just had to be endured, though. She focused on the thought of her sister's smiling face and her new baby nephew as the plane slowly pulled onto the runway.

Which of the following is Elizabeth least likely to do in the future?

A)   Take a flight to her brother's wedding.

B)   Apply for a job as a flight attendant.

C)   Never board an airplane again.

D)   Get sick on an airplane.

Answer: It's clear from the passage that Elizabeth hates flying, but it willing to endure it for the sake of visiting her family. Thus, it seems likely that she would be willing to get on a plane for her brother's wedding, making A) and C) incorrect answers. The passage also explicitly tells us that she feels sick on planes, so D) is likely to happen. We can infer, though, that she would not enjoy being on an airplane for work, so she's very unlikely to apply for a job as a flight attendant, which is choice B).

Word and Phrase Meaning Through Context

On the Reading section you may also be asked to provide definitions or intended meanings for words within passages. You may have never encountered some of these words before the test, but there are tricks you can use to figure out what they mean.

Context Clues

The most fundamental vocabulary skill is using the context in which a word is used to determine its meaning. Your ability to observe sentences closely is extremely useful when it comes to understanding new vocabulary words.

There are two types of context that can help you understand the meaning of unfamiliar words: situational context and sentence context. Regardless of which context is present, these types of questions are not really testing your knowledge of vocabulary; rather, they test your ability to comprehend the meaning of a word through its usage.

Situational context is context that is presented by the setting or circumstances in which a word or phrase occurs. **Sentence context** occurs within the specific sentence that contains the vocabulary word. To figure out words using sentence context clues, you should first determine the most important words in the sentence.

There are four types of clues that can help you understand context, and therefore the meaning of a word:

- **Restatement** clues occur when the definition of the word is clearly stated in the sentence.
- **Positive/negative** clues can tell you whether a word has a positive or negative meaning.
- **Contrast** clues include the opposite meaning of a word. Words like *but*, *on the other hand*, and *however* are tip-offs that a sentence contains a contrast clue.
- **Specific detail** clues provide a precise detail that can help you understand the meaning of the word.

It is important to remember that more than one of these clues can be present in the same sentence. The more there are, the easier it will be to determine the meaning of the word. For example, the following sentence uses both restatement and positive/negative clues: *Janet suddenly found herself destitute, so poor she could barely afford to eat.* The second part of the sentence clearly indicates that *destitute* is a negative word. It also restates the meaning: very poor.

Examples

I had a hard time reading her *illegible* handwriting.
A)   neat
B)   unsafe
C)   sloppy
D)   educated

Answer: Already, you know that this sentence is discussing something that is hard to read. Look at the word that *illegible* is describing: handwriting. Based on context clues, you can tell that *illegible* means that her handwriting is hard to read.

Next, look at the answer choices. Choice A), *neat*, is obviously a wrong answer because neat handwriting would not be difficult to read. Choices B) and D), *unsafe* and *educated*, don't make sense. Therefore, choice C), *sloppy*, is the best answer.

The dog was *dauntless* in the face of danger, braving the fire to save the girl trapped inside the building.
A)   difficult
B)   fearless
C)   imaginative
D)   startled

Answer: Demonstrating bravery in the face of danger would be B) *fearless*. In this case, the restatement clue (*braving the fire*) tells you exactly what the word means.

> Beth did not spend any time preparing for the test, but Tyrone kept a *rigorous* study schedule.
> A)   strict
> B)   loose
> C)   boring
> D)   strange

Answer: In this case, the contrast word *but* tells us that Tyrone studied in a different way than Beth, which means it's a contrast clue. If Beth did not study hard, then Tyrone did. The best answer, therefore, is choice A).

Analyzing Words

As you no doubt know, determining the meaning of a word can be more complicated than just looking in a dictionary. A word might have more than one **denotation**, or definition; which one the author intends can only be judged by looking at the surrounding text. For example, the word *quack* can refer to the sound a duck makes, or to a person who publicly pretends to have a qualification which he or she does not actually possess.

A word may also have different **connotations**, which are the implied meanings and emotion a word evokes in the reader. For example, a cubicle is a simply a walled desk in an office, but for many the word implies a constrictive, uninspiring workplace. Connotations can vary greatly between cultures and even between individuals.

Lastly, authors might make use of **figurative language**, which is the use of a word to imply something other than the word's literal definition. This is often done by comparing two things. If you say *I felt like a butterfly when I got a new haircut*, the listener knows you don't resemble an insect but instead felt beautiful and transformed.

Word Structure

Although you are not expected to know every word in the English language for your test, you will need the ability to use deductive reasoning to find the choice that is the best match for the word in question, which is why we are going to explain how to break a word into its parts to determine its meaning. Many words can be broken down into three main parts:

prefix – root – suffix

Roots are the building blocks of all words. Every word is either a root itself or has a root. Just as a plant cannot grow without roots, neither can vocabulary, because a word must have a root to give it meaning. The root is what is left when you strip away all the prefixes and suffixes from a word. For example, in the word *unclear*, if you take away the prefix *un-*, you have the root *clear*.

Roots are not always recognizable words, because they generally come from Latin or Greek words, such as *nat*, a Latin root meaning born. The word *native*, which means a person born in a referenced placed, comes from this root, so does the word *prenatal*, meaning before birth. It's important to keep in mind, however, that roots do not always match the exact definitions of words, and they can have several different spellings.

Prefixes are syllables added to the beginning of a word and **suffixes** are syllables added to the end of the word. Both carry assigned meanings and can be attached to a word to completely change the word's meaning or to enhance the word's original meaning.

Let's use the word prefix itself as an example: *fix* means to place something securely and *pre-* means before. Therefore, *prefix* means to place something before or in front. Now let's look at a suffix: in the word *feminism*, *femin* is a root which means female. The suffix *-ism* means act, practice, or process. Thus, *feminism* is the process of establishing equal rights for women.

Although you cannot determine the meaning of a word by a prefix or suffix alone, you can use this knowledge to eliminate answer choices; understanding whether the word is positive or negative can give you the partial meaning of the word.

Questions 1 – 4 are based on the following passage:

From *"On Lying Awake at Night"* by Stewart Edward White *(public domain)*:

About once in so often you are due to lie awake at night. Why this is so I have never been able to discover. It apparently comes from no predisposing uneasiness of indigestion, no rashness in the matter of too much tea or tobacco, no excitation of unusual incident or stimulating conversation. In fact, you turn in with the expectation of rather a good night's rest. Almost at once the little noises of the forest grow larger, blend in the hollow bigness of the first drowse; your thoughts drift idly back and forth between reality and dream; when—*snap!*—you are broad awake!

For, unlike mere insomnia, lying awake at night in the woods is pleasant. The eager, nervous straining for sleep gives way to a delicious indifference. You do not care. Your mind is cradled in an exquisite poppy-suspension of judgment and of thought. Impressions slip vaguely into your consciousness and as vaguely out again. Sometimes they stand stark and naked for your inspection; sometimes they lose themselves in the mist of half-sleep. Always they lay soft velvet fingers on the drowsy imagination, so that in their caressing you feel the vaster spaces from which they have come. Peaceful-brooding your *faculties* receive. Hearing, sight, smell—all are preternaturally keen to whatever of sound and sight and woods perfume is abroad through the night; and yet at the same time active appreciation dozes, so these things lie on it sweet and cloying like fallen rose-leaves.

Nothing is more fantastically unreal to tell about, nothing more concretely real to experience, than this undernote of the quick water. And when you do lie awake at night, it is always making its unobtrusive appeal. Gradually its hypnotic spell works. The distant chimes ring louder and nearer as you cross the borderland of sleep. And then outside the tent some little woods noise snaps the thread. An owl hoots, a whippoorwill cries, a twig cracks beneath the cautious prowl of some night creature—at once the yellow sunlit French meadows puff away—you are staring at the blurred image of the moon spraying through the texture of your tent.

(You have cast from you with the warm blanket the drowsiness of dreams. A coolness, physical and spiritual, bathes you from head to foot. All your senses are keyed to the last vibrations. You hear the littler night prowlers; you glimpse the greater. A faint, searching woods perfume of dampness greets your nostrils. And somehow, mysteriously, in a manner not to be understood, the forces of the world seem in suspense, as though a touch might crystallize infinite possibilities into infinite power and motion. But the touch lacks. The forces hover on the edge of action, unheeding the little noises. In all humbleness and awe, you are a dweller of the Silent Places.

The night wind from the river, or from the open spaces of the wilds, chills you after a time. You begin to think of your blankets. In a few moments you roll yourself in their soft wool. Instantly it is morning.

And, strange to say, you have not to pay by going through the day unrefreshed. You may feel like turning in at eight instead of nine, and you may fall asleep with unusual promptitude, but your journey will begin clear-headedly, proceed springily, and end with much in reserve. No languor, no dull headache, no exhaustion, follows your experience. For this once your two hours of sleep have been as effective as nine.

1. In Paragraph 2, "faculties" is used to mean:
    a) Teachers.
    b) Senses.
    c) Imaginations.
    d) Capacities.

2. The author's opinion of insomnia is that:
    a) It is not a problem because nights without sleep are refreshing.
    b) It can happen more often when sleeping in the woods because of the noises in nature.
    c) It is generally unpleasant, but sometimes can be hypnotic.
    d) It is the best way to cultivate imagination.

3. By "strange to say" in Paragraph 6, the author means:
    a) The experience of the night before had an unreal quality.
    b) The language used in describing the night before is not easily understood.
    c) It is not considered acceptable to express the opinion the author expresses.
    d) Contrary to expectations, one is well-rested after the night before.

4. How is this essay best characterized?
    a) A playful examination of a common medical problem.
    b) A curious look at both sides of an issue.
    c) A fanciful description of the author's experience.
    d) A horrific depiction of night hallucinations.

Questions 5-10 are based on the following passages:

Passage One
An excerpt from the essay *"Tradition and the Individual Talent"* by T.S. Eliot (public domain):

No poet, no artist of any art, has his complete meaning alone. His significance, his appreciation is the appreciation of his relation to the dead poets and artists. You cannot value him alone; you must set him, for contrast and comparison, among the dead. I mean this as a principle of aesthetic, not merely historical, criticism. The necessity that he shall conform, that he shall cohere, is not one-sided; what happens when a new work of art is created is something that happens simultaneously to all the works of art which preceded it. The existing monuments form an ideal order among themselves, which is modified by the introduction of the new (the really new) work of art among them. The existing order is complete before the new work arrives; for order to persist after the supervention of novelty, the *whole* existing order must be, if ever so slightly, altered; and so the relations, proportions, values of each work of art toward the whole are readjusted; and this is conformity between the old and the new. Whoever has approved this idea of order, of the form of European, of English literature, will not find it preposterous that the past should be altered by the present as much as the present is directed by the past. And the poet who is aware of this will be aware of great difficulties and responsibilities.

Passage Two
An excerpt from the Clive Bell's seminal art history book "Art" (public domain):

To criticize a work of art historically is to play the science-besotted fool. No more disastrous theory ever issued from the brain of a charlatan than that of evolution in art. Giotto[1] did not creep, a grub, that Titian[2] might flaunt, a butterfly. To think of a man's art as leading on to the art of someone else is to misunderstand it. To praise or abuse or be interested in a work of art because it leads or does not lead to another work of art is to treat it as though it were not a work of art. The connection of one work of art with another may have everything to do with history: it has nothing to do with appreciation. So soon as we begin to consider a work as anything else than an end in itself we leave the world of art. Though the development of painting from Giotto to Titian may be interesting historically, it cannot affect the value of any particular picture: aesthetically, it is of no consequence whatever. Every work of art must be judged on its own merits.

5. In Passage One, the word "cohere" is used to most closely mean:
    a) To be congruous with.
    b) To supplant.
    c) To imitate.
    d) To overhaul.
    e) To deviate from.

6. In Passage Two, the author alludes to a butterfly to contradict which concept?
    a) The theory of evolution is responsible for the discipline of art criticism.
    b) Scientific knowledge is not necessary to understand paintings.
    c) Artists who show off are doomed to be criticized.
    d) Art which finds inspiration in nature is the highest form of art.
    e) Titian's art is beautiful as a result of the horrible art that came before.

7. The author of Passage One would be most likely to support:
    a) An artist who imitated the great works of the past.
    b) An art critic who relied solely on evaluating the aesthetics of new art.
    c) A historian who studied the aesthetic evolution of art.
    d) An artist who was also a scientist.
    e) An artist who shouldered the burden of creating something new, while affecting the old, in the world of art.

8. The meaning of the sentence "To praise or abuse or be interested in a work of art because it leads or does not lead to another work of art is to treat it as though it were not a work of art" in Passage 2 means:
    a) Works of art cannot be judged primarily by their relation to one another.
    b) One should not vandalize works of art.
    c) It is necessary to understand how one work of art leads to another in order to judge it.
    d) Works of art must be treated with respect.
    e) Understanding works of art is reliant on seeing them on a historical scale.

9. The author of Passage One would likely agree with which of the following statements?
    a) The past is a monument that is unalterable by the present.

---
[1] Giotto was an Italian painter during the Middle Ages.
[2] Titian was an Italian painter during the Renaissance.

b) Historical knowledge is entirely separate from artistic knowledge.
c) To understand a novel written in the twentieth century, it is necessary to have some knowledge of nineteenth century literature.
d) Painters of Italian descent are all related to one another.
e) One cannot be a scholar of literary history without also being a scholar of scientific thought.

10. The authors of both passages would likely agree with which of the following statements?
   a) An aesthetic judgment is the greatest possible approach to art criticism.
   b) Knowledge of history compromises one's ability to criticize works of art.
   c) The painter Titian was able to create his art as a consequence of the art which came before his time.
   d) It is imperative to understand the progression from one work of art to another.
   e) Not all works of art are consequential.

Questions 11 and 12 are based on the following passage:

Excerpt from Anne Walker's "*A Matter of Proportion*," a short science-fiction story published in 1959 (public domain). In this excerpt, one character tells another about an injured man who is planning a secret operation:

On the way, he filled in background. Scott had been living out of the hospital in a small apartment, enjoying as much liberty as he could manage. He had equipment so he could stump around, and an antique car specially equipped. He wasn't complimentary about them. Orthopedic products had to be: unreliable, hard to service, unsightly, intricate, and uncomfortable. If they also squeaked and cut your clothes, fine!

Having to plan every move with an eye on weather and a dozen other factors, he developed an uncanny foresight. Yet he had to improvise at a moment's notice. With life a continuous high-wire act, he trained every surviving fiber to precision, dexterity, and tenacity. Finally, he avoided help. Not pride, self-preservation; the compulsively helpful have rarely the wit to ask before rushing in to knock you on your face, so he learned to bide his time till the horizon was clear of beaming simpletons. Also, he found an interest in how far he could go.

11. Why does Scott primarily avoid the help of others?
   a) He has found that he is usually better off without it.
   b) He does not want to rely on other people for anything.
   c) He is doing experiments to test his own limits.
   d) He is working on a secret operation and cannot risk discovery.
   e) He does not realize that he needs assistance.

12. "Orthopedic" in paragraph one most nearly means:
   a) Uncomfortable.
   b) Dangerous.
   c) Corrective.
   d) Enhanced.
   e) Complicated.

Excerpt from Rennie W. Doane's *"Insects and Disease,"* a popular science account published in 1910 (public domain):

It has been estimated that there are about four thousand species or kinds of Protozoans, about twenty-five thousand species of Mollusks, about ten thousand species of birds, about three thousand five hundred species of mammals, and from two hundred thousand to one million species of insects, or from two to five times as many kinds of insects as all other animals combined.

Not only do the insects preponderate in number of species, but the number of individuals belonging to many of the species is absolutely beyond our comprehension. Try to count the number of little green aphis on a single infested rose-bush, or on a cabbage plant; guess at the number of mosquitoes issuing each day from a good breeding-pond; estimate the number of scale insects on a single square inch of a tree badly infested with San José scale; then try to think how many more bushes or trees or ponds may be breeding their millions just as these and you will only begin to comprehend the meaning of this statement.

As long as these myriads of insects keep, in what we are pleased to call their proper place, we care not for their numbers and think little of them except as some student points out some wonderful thing about their structure, life-history or adaptations. But since the dawn of history we find accounts to show that insects have not always kept to their proper sphere but have insisted at various times and in various ways in interfering with man's plans and wishes, and on account of their excessive numbers the results have often been most disastrous.

Insects cause an annual loss to the people of the United States of over $1,000,000,000. Grain fields are devastated; orchards and gardens are destroyed or seriously affected; forests are made waste places and in scores of other ways these little pests which do not keep in their proper places are exacting this tremendous tax from our people. These things have been known and recognized for centuries, and scores of volumes have been written about the insects and their ways and of methods of combating them.

Yellow fever, while not so widespread as malaria, is more fatal and therefore more terrorizing. Its presence and spread are due entirely to a single species of mosquito, *Stegomyia calopus*. While this species is usually restricted to tropical or semi-tropical regions it sometimes makes its appearance in places farther north, especially in summer time, where it may thrive for a time. The adult mosquito is black, conspicuously marked with white. The legs and abdomen are banded with white and on the thorax is a series of white lines which in well-preserved specimens distinctly resembles a lyre. These mosquitoes are essentially domestic insects, for they are very rarely found except in houses or in their immediate vicinity. Once they enter a room they will scarcely leave it except to lay their eggs in a near-by cistern, water-pot, or some other convenient place.

Their habit of biting in the daytime has gained for them the name of "day mosquitoes" to distinguish them from the night feeders. But they will bite at night as well as by day and many other species are not at all adverse to a daylight meal, if the opportunity offers, so this habit is not distinctive. The recognition of these facts has a distinct bearing in the methods adopted to prevent the spread of yellow fever. There are no striking characters or habits in the larval or pupal stages that would enable us to distinguish without careful examination this species from other similar forms with which it might be associated. For some time it was claimed that this species would breed only in clean water, but it has been found that it is not nearly so particular, some even claiming that it prefers foul water. I have seen them breeding in countless thousands in company with *Stegomyia scutellaris* and *Culex fatigans* in the sewer drains in Tahiti in the streets of

Papeete. As the larva feed largely on bacteria one would expect to find them in exactly such places where the bacteria are of course abundant. The fact that they are able to live in any kind of water and in a very small amount of it well adapts them to their habits of living about dwellings.

13. Why does the author list the amounts of different species of organisms in paragraph 1?
   a) To illustrate the vast number of species in the world.
   b) To demonstrate authority on the subject of insects.
   c) To establish the relative importance of mollusks and birds.
   d) To demonstrate the proportion of insects to other organisms.

14. What does the author use "their proper place" at the beginning of paragraph 3?
   a) The author is alluding to people's tendency to view insects as largely irrelevant to their lives.
   b) The author feels that insects belong only outdoors.
   c) The author wants the reader to feel superior to insects.
   d) The author is warning that insects can evolve to affect the course of human events.

15. This passage can be characterized primarily as:
   a) Pedantic.
   b) Droll.
   c) Informative.
   d) Abstract.
   e) Cautionary.

16. The main idea of this passage is best summarized as:
   a) Disease-carrying mosquitoes have adapted to best live near human settlements.
   b) Insects can have a detrimental effect on the economy by destroying crops.
   c) Insects are numerous in both types of species and individuals within a species.
   d) Although people do not always consider insects consequential, they can have substantial effects on human populations.

17. The use of "domestic" in Paragraph 5 most nearly means:
   a) Originating in the United States.
   b) Under the care of and bred by humans.
   c) Fearful of the outdoors.
   d) Living near human homes.

18. Which of the following ideas would best belong in this passage?
   a) An historical example of the effect a yellow fever outbreak had on civilization.
   b) A biological explanation of how diseases are transmitted from insects to humans.
   c) A reference to the numbers of insects which live far away from human habitation.
   d) Strategies for the prevention of yellow fever and malaria.

The collapse of the arbitrage[3] firm Long-Term Capital Management (LTCM) in 1998 is explained by a host of different factors: its investments were based on a high level of leverage, for example, and it was significantly impacted by Russia's default on the ruble. However, sociologist Donald MacKenzie maintains that the main factor in LTCM's demise was that, like all arbitrage firms, it was subjected to the sociological phenomena of the arbitrage community; namely, imitation. Arbitrageurs, who are generally known to one another as members of a specific subset of the financial society, use decision-making strategies based not only on mathematical models or pure textbook reason, but also based upon their feelings and gut reactions toward the financial market and on the actions of their peers. This imitation strategy leads to the overlapping "super portfolio," which creates an inherent instability that leads to collapse, the most infamous example being LTCM.

The public opinion of the partners of the firm in 1998 was that it had acted cavalierly with borrowed capital. However, in actuality the firm's strategy was exceedingly conservative, with a diversified portfolio, overestimated risks, and carefully hedged investments. The firm even tested tactics for dealing with financial emergencies such as the collapse of the European Monetary Union. Before the 1998 crisis, those in LTCM were never accused of recklessness. Nor were they, as is sometimes explained, overly reliant on mathematical models. The statistical hubris explanation falters under MacKenzie's evidence that John Meriwether and the others who ran the firm made their investment decisions based more upon their intricate understandings of the arbitrage market rather than upon the pure results of mathematical analyses. The financial instability that was created was not the result of the decision-making of one firm; but rather, the collective patterns of decision-making of all of the arbitrage firms at the time.

The infamy of LTCM worked against the company. LTCM was composed of some of the most eminent minds in finance and it made devastating profits for the first few years that it was running. This led to imitation by other arbitrageurs who viewed the investments of LTCM as nearly sure bets. This type of replication of investment portfolios is not surprising, considering that arbitrageurs are all looking for similar types of pricing discrepancies and anomalies to exploit. The structure of arbitrageurs as a unique subset of the financial community who are largely personally known to one another further contributes to this phenomenon. Because of these factors over time the various players in the field of arbitrage created overlapping investments which MacKenzie dubs a "super portfolio." While LTCM alone may have created a geographically and industrially diverse portfolio, across the discipline of arbitrage as a whole capital flocked to similar investments.

Because of this super portfolio trend, multiple arbitrageurs were affected by the price changes of different assets caused by the actions of single independent firms. MacKenzie cites the example of the takeover of the investment bank Salomon Brothers by the Travelers Corporation. Salomon Brothers' portfolio, now under the management of someone who disliked the risks of arbitrage trading, liquidated its positions, which drove down the prices of assets in the markets in which it operated. The liquidation of the holdings of such a prominent player in the arbitrage game negatively affected the positions of every other firm that had a stake in those markets, including, of course, LTCM. This also illustrates the other sociological side of MacKenzie's argument: that arbitrageurs are subject to irrational internal pressures to cut their losses before their investments play out, which one of his interview subjects terms "queasiness" when faced with a stretch of losses.

---

[3] "Arbitrage" is a financial strategy which takes advantage of the temporary price differences of a single asset in different markets.

19. The second paragraph of this passage primarily aims to:
   a) Explain that recklessness with borrowed capital is never profitable.
   b) Explore the factors ultimately responsible for the demise of the arbitrage firm Long-Term Capital Management.
   c) Demonstrate how the practice of arbitrage works.
   d) Laud the use of statistical models in calculating financial risks.
   e) Present and dismiss several theories of the collapse of Long-Term Capital Management.

20. In paragraph 2, "devastating" is used to mean:
   a) Destructive.
   b) Attractive.
   c) Blasphemous.
   d) Considerable.
   e) Appalling.

21. The final paragraph in this passage:
   a) Refutes the argument presented in the second paragraph of the passage.
   b) Gives a logical example of the phenomenon described in the introductory first paragraph of the passage.
   c) Contains an ardent plea against the passage of arbitrage.
   d) Gives a step-by-step account of the demise of Long-Term Capital Management.
   e) Argues that an understanding of sociology is crucial to successful financial practice.

22. Which of the following is a best description of the author's approach to the topic?
   a) Impassioned exposition.
   b) Curious exploration.
   c) Gleeful detection.
   d) Disgusted condemnation.
   e) Serene indifference.

23. Which of the following most accurately summarizes the author's thesis?
   a) If Long-Term Capital Management had developed a superportfolio, it would not have collapsed.
   b) Financial markets are inherently instable because those who participate in them are subject to human faults.
   c) Arbitrage firms should always endeavor to have geographically and industrially diverse investments.
   d) Long-Term Capital Management collapsed because arbitrageurs across the industry were investing in the same things, which caused instability.
   e) Long-Term Capital Management was run by financiers who were reckless and overly dependent on mathematical models, which is why it collapsed.

24. "Hubris" in paragraph 2 most likely means:
   a) Mathematical model.
   b) Reliance.
   c) Arrogance.
   d) Denial.
   e) Mistake.

25. Which of the following facts would undermine the main argument of the passage?
   a) The European Monetary Union was close to collapse in 1998.
   b) Some arbitrage firms steered clear of the practice of superportfolios.
   c) The Travelers Corporation was run by financiers who favored the practice of arbitrage.
   d) Arbitrageurs rarely communicate with one another or get information from the same source.
   e) Mathematical models used in finance in the 1990s were highly reliable.

26. Which of the following supports the argument made in the third paragraph?
   a) A detailed outline of the statistical models used by Long-Term Capital Management to make decisions.
   b) An explanation of how other arbitrage firms were able to learn the tactics practiced by Long-Term Capital Management.
   c) Examples of the differences between different investment portfolios of arbitrage firms.
   d) An outline of sociological theories about decision-making processes.
   e) A map showing the geographical diversity of arbitrage investors.

Questions 27 – 36 are based on a long passage excerpted from Robert Louis Stevenson's classic novel ___Treasure Island___ *(public domain). In this passage, the narrator tells about an old sailor staying at his family's inn.*

He had taken me aside one day and promised me a silver fourpenny on the first of every month if I would only keep my "weather-eye open for a seafaring man with one leg" and let him know the moment he appeared. Often enough when the first of the month came round and I applied to him for my wage, he would only blow through his nose at me and stare me down, but before the week was out he was sure to think better of it, bring me my fourpenny piece, and repeat his orders to look out for "the seafaring man with one leg."

How that personage haunted my dreams, I need scarcely tell you. On stormy nights, when the wind shook the four corners of the house and the surf roared along the cove and up the cliffs, I would see him in a thousand forms, and with a thousand diabolical expressions. Now the leg would be cut off at the knee, now at the hip; now he was a monstrous kind of a creature who had never had but the one leg, and that in the middle of his body. To see him leap and run and pursue me over hedge and ditch was the worst of nightmares. And altogether I paid pretty dear for my monthly fourpenny piece, in the shape of these abominable fancies.

But though I was so terrified by the idea of the seafaring man with one leg, I was far less afraid of the captain himself than anybody else who knew him. There were nights when he took a deal more rum and water than his head would carry; and then he would sometimes sit and sing his wicked, old, wild sea-songs, minding nobody; but sometimes he would call for glasses round and force all the trembling company to listen to his stories or bear a chorus to his singing. Often I have heard the house shaking with "Yo-ho-ho, and a bottle of rum," all the neighbors joining in for dear life, with the fear of death upon them, and each singing louder than the other to avoid remark. For in these fits he was the most overriding companion ever known; he would slap his hand on the table for silence all round; he would fly up in a passion of anger at a question, or sometimes because none was put, and so he judged the company was not following his story. Nor would he allow anyone to leave the inn till he had drunk himself sleepy and reeled off to bed.

His stories were what frightened people worst of all. Dreadful stories they were—about hanging, and walking the plank, and storms at sea, and the Dry Tortugas, and wild deeds and places on the Spanish Main. By his own account he must have lived his life among some of the wickedest men that God ever allowed upon the sea, and the language in which he told these stories shocked our plain country people almost as much as the crimes that he described. My father was always saying the inn would be ruined, for people would soon cease coming there to be tyrannized over and put down, and sent shivering to their beds; but I really believe his presence did us good. People were frightened at the time, but on looking back they rather liked it; it was a fine excitement in a quiet country life, and there was even a party of the younger men who pretended to admire him, calling him a "true sea-dog" and a "real old salt" and such like names, and saying there was the sort of man that made England terrible at sea.

In one way, indeed, he bade fair to ruin us, for he kept on staying week after week, and at last month after month, so that all the money had been long exhausted, and still my father never plucked up the heart to insist on having more. If ever he mentioned it, the captain blew through his nose so loudly that you might say he roared, and stared my poor father out of the room. I have seen him wringing his hands after such a rebuff, and I am sure the annoyance and the terror he lived in must have greatly hastened his early and unhappy death.

27. The purpose of Paragraph 3 is to:
    a) Illustrate how others view the captain.
    b) Explain the narrator's relationship with the captain.
    c) Give more background information about the inn where the narrator lives.
    d) Recount old seafaring lore.
    e) Explain why the captain is staying at this inn.

28. Which paragraph serves to evoke the life lived by sailors at sea?
    a) 1.
    b) 2.
    c) 3.
    d) 4.
    e) 5.

29. "Diabolical" in Paragraph 2 most nearly means:
    a) Angry.
    b) Judgmental.
    c) Contorted.
    d) Fiendish.
    e) Stoic.

30. What kind of character does the author reveal the captain to be the third paragraph?
    a) Temperamental.
    b) Generous.
    c) Jocund.
    d) Mysterious.
    e) Reserved.

31. What does the author reveal about the narrator in Paragraph 5?
- a) The narrator is afraid of the captain.
- b) The narrator is eager to go to sea.
- c) The narrator was often angry and annoyed.
- d) The narrator grew up in poverty.
- e) The narrator lost his father at an early age.

32. "Tyrannized" in Paragraph 4 is used to mean:
- a) Cajoled.
- b) Bullied.
- c) Frightened.
- d) Robbed.
- e) Ejected.

33. Which of the following statements about this passage is false?
- a) It is unclear whether the "seafaring man with one leg" actually exists.
- b) The narrator harbors a serious grudge against the captain.
- c) The narrator is interested in the captain's stories.
- d) The story takes place near the ocean.
- e) Most people who populate the story are afraid of the captain.

34. According to the captain, all of the following are hazards which can be encountered at sea EXCEPT:
- a) Hangings.
- b) Wicked men.
- c) Walking the plank.
- d) Storms.
- e) Sea monsters.

35. It can be inferred from the passage that:
- a) Singing was frowned upon in the community.
- b) The narrator never knew his mother.
- c) The narrator admired the captain.
- d) The captain is afraid of the seafaring man with one leg.
- e) The narrator went on to become a pirate.

36. By "they rather liked it" at the end of Paragraph 4, the author most closely means:
- a) The patrons of the inn enjoyed singing.
- b) The captain and others appreciated the rum available for sale at the inn.
- c) The narrator and his friends liked the stories the captain told.
- d) The captain provided entertainment at the inn, which would otherwise be boring.
- e) The narrator's parents liked having the captain around.

Questions 37 – 40 are based on a short passage excerpted from the introduction to The Best American Humorous Short Stories, edited by Alexander Jessup (public domain).

No book is duller than a book of jokes, for what is refreshing in small doses becomes nauseating when perused in large assignments. Humor in literature is at its best not when served merely by itself but when presented along with other ingredients of literary force in order to give a wide representation of life. Therefore "professional literary humorists," as they may be called, have not been much considered in making up this collection. In the history of American humor there are three names which stand out more prominently than all others before Mark Twain, who, however, also belongs to a wider classification: "Josh Billings" (Henry Wheeler Shaw, 1815-1885), "Petroleum V. Nasby" (David Ross Locke, 1833-1888), and "Artemus Ward" (Charles Farrar Browne, 1834-1867). In the history of American humor these names rank high; in the field of American literature and the American short story they do not rank so high. I have found nothing of theirs that was first-class both as humor and as short story. Perhaps just below these three should be mentioned George Horatio Derby (1823-1861), author of *Phoenixiana* (1855) and the *Squibob Papers* (1859), who wrote under the name "John Phoenix." As has been justly said, "Derby, Shaw, Locke and Browne carried to an extreme numerous tricks already invented by earlier American humorists, particularly the tricks of gigantic exaggeration and calm-faced mendacity, but they are plainly in the main channel of American humor, which had its origin in the first comments of settlers upon the conditions of the frontier, long drew its principal inspiration from the differences between that frontier and the more settled and compact regions of the country, and reached its highest development in Mark Twain, in his youth a child of the American frontier, admirer and imitator of Derby and Browne, and eventually a man of the world and one of its greatest humorists."

37. The author of this passage would disagree with all of the following statements EXCEPT:
   a) To be a successful storyteller, one must also be a professional literary humorist.
   b) Mark Twain is the most prominent American humorist.
   c) Lying with a straight face is a literary humorist device which had just been invented at the time this was published.
   d) The best joke books are the longest ones.
   e) Professional literary humorism is the highest form of writing.

38. The purpose of this passage is to:
   a) Scorn humorous writing as lesser than storytelling.
   b) Explain how writers use humorous literary devices.
   c) Provide contextual information about the landscape of American humorous writing.
   d) Make a case for the appreciation of the humorists Henry Shaw and David Locke.
   e) Deny the historical roots of American literary humor.

39. The word "prominently" in line four most closely means:
   a) Extravagantly.
   b) Inconspicuously.
   c) Significantly.
   d) Comically.
   e) Conceitedly.

40. Which of the following best summarizes the author's theory of the origins of American humorous writing?
   a) It started as a way of breaking away from British literary humor.
   b) It grew hand-in-hand with American storytelling.
   c) It was founded by Mark Twain.
   d) It was inspired by the differences between settlements and the frontier.
   e) It began with exaggerations and mendacity.

1. b)	21. b)
2. c)	22. b)
3. d)	23. d)
4. c)	24. c)
5. a)	25. d)
6. e)	26. b)
7. e)	27. a)
8. a)	28. d)
9. c)	29. d)
10. e)	30. a)
11. a)	31. e)
12. c)	32. b)
13. d)	33. b)
14. a)	34. e)
15. c)	35. c)
16. d)	36. d)
17. d)	37. b)
18. a)	38. c)
19. e)	39. c)
20. d)	40. d)

Chapter 2: Writing

The knowledge just covered in the reading chapter of this book will come in handy during this section as well. In the writing portion of the exam, you will need to demonstrate your competency in both the usage and mechanics of the English language, as well as rhetorical skills.

The **usage/mechanics questions** cover the following concepts:

- **Punctuation:** Apostrophes, colons, semi-colons, commas, dashes, hyphens, quotation marks, parentheses, and their functions in clarifying the meaning of text selections.

- **Basic Grammar:** Verbs, adverbs, adjectives, subject-verb agreement, pronoun-antecedent agreement, and the proper use of connectives.

- **Sentence Structure:** Clauses, modifiers, parallelism, consistency in tense, and point-of-view.

Remember the reading section? The **rhetorical questions** are quite similar. You will be given a passage to read, with questions covering either the entire passage, or separate parts. You will demonstrate your knowledge of:

- **Strategy:** The author's choice of supporting material – if is it effective, applicable, and ample in quality and quantity.

- **Style:** The best choice of adjectives, word order, or alternative wording that most concisely articulates an idea.

- **Organization:** Sentence arrangement within a paragraph, paragraph arrangement within the passage, the need for further information, and the presence of unnecessary information.

Tips

As with all the section tests, you have to know your English grammar. This exam will not be unjustly 'sneaky,' but you do have to be observant and thorough enough to catch errors. Here are some tips to help improve your score.

The Three Main No-No's.
There are three main things the test is stringent about:

1. **Redundancy** (repetitious text or words).

2. **Irrelevance** (words or ideas not directly or logically associated with the purpose or main idea).

3. **Wordiness** (drawing out a sentence).

Peruse the entire passage paragraph before answering any of the questions.

Many study guides will tell you not to read the entire passage before answering the usage/mechanics questions; however, that approach lends to a greater possibility of error. The overall meaning or purpose of the paragraph can change the propriety of the highlighted text. For example, looking at just the sentence containing the highlighted word group may cause you to misinterpret the intended parallels or point of view.

Read every word of every question.
Don't assume that you know what is being asked after reading the first few words. Remember, one word at the end of a sentence can change the entire meaning.

Read all the answer choices before making a selection.
Some choices will be partially correct (pertaining to a part, but not all, of the passage) and are intended to catch the eye of the sloppy tester. Note the differences between your answer choices; sometimes they are very subtle.

Understand transitions.
The exam will require you to recognize the shortest, most proper way to go from one sentence or paragraph to another.

Familiarize yourself with various styles of writing.
The passages may be excerpts from anything: poetry, cause/effect essays, comparison /contrast essays, definition essays, description essays, narration essays, persuasive essays, or process analysis essays.

Learn the directions.
Knowing the directions before test day saves valuable minutes. It enables you to glance quickly at the directions and start answering questions.

And, most importantly, review! Most people cannot learn sentence rules by memorization, like they do math or science. Instead, the best way to learn how sentences fit together is by reading! Studying the following terms and rules will help a great deal.

Syntax

"Syntax" refers to the rules for the formation of grammatical sentences in a language. (That definition, while correct, is pretty stuffy. Basically, "syntax" means "sentence structure.")

It's very easy to understand why syntax is important. In order to convey meaningful information in a way that makes sense, sentences need to comply with the rules of grammar. Most readers and speakers have a general understanding of these rules; it's crucial for you to demonstrate syntactical competency as well.

Let's look at an example.

> "When Heidi woke up in the morning, she noticed three things which disturbed her greatly: the first being that she was a ghost."

But what if we started the sentence this way?

"The first being that she was a ghost: she noticed three things when Heidi woke up which disturbed her greatly."

After reading this sentence, you would probably be utterly confused and, most likely, unwilling to continue reading. Why would you have this reaction? Because the sentence doesn't make grammatical sense.

Now the above example is very easy. But chances are that the questions on the exam may be a bit harder. Therefore, it's important that you understand the top five grammatical rules:

1. Sentences that maintain the subject-verb-object order are more readable than those which do not.

2. When you can, place the subject and the verb close together in a sentence.

3. Keep modifiers and the words that they modify close together in a sentence.

4. Try to put people in the subject position in a sentence.

5. Put old information first in a sentence and new information last.

Nouns, Pronouns, Verbs, Adjectives, and Adverbs

Nouns
Nouns are people, places, or things. They are typically the subject of a sentence. For example, "The hospital was very clean." The noun is "hospital;" it is the "place."

Pronouns
Pronouns essentially "replace" nouns. This allows a sentence to not sound repetitive. Take the sentence: "Sam stayed home from school because Sam was not feeling well." The word "Sam" appears twice in the same sentence. Instead, you can use a pronoun and say, "Sam stayed at home because *he* did not feel well." Sounds much better, right?

Most Common Pronouns:

- I, me, mine, my.

- You, your, yours.

- He, him, his.

- She, her, hers.

- It, its.

- We, us, our, ours.

- They, them, their, theirs.

35

Verbs

Remember the old commercial, "Verb: It's what you do"? That sums up verbs in a nutshell! Verbs are the "action" of a sentence; verbs "do" things.

They can, however, be quite tricky. Depending on the subject of a sentence, the tense of the word (past, present, future, etc.), and whether or not they are regular or irregular, verbs have many variations.

> **Example:** "He runs to second base." The verb is "runs." This is a "regular verb."

> **Example**: "I am 7 years old." The verb in this case is "am." This is an "irregular verb."

As mentioned, verbs must use the correct tense – and that tense must remain the same throughout the sentence. "I was baking cookies and eat some dough." That sounded strange, didn't it? That's because the two verbs "baking" and "eat" are presented in different tenses. "Was baking" occurred in the past; "eat," on the other hand, occurs in the present. Instead, it should be "**ate** some dough."

Adjectives

Adjectives are words that describe a noun and give more information. Take the sentence: "The boy hit the ball." If you want to know more about the noun "boy," then you could use an adjective to describe it. "The **little** boy hit the ball." An adjective simply provides more information about a noun or subject in a sentence.

Adverbs

For some reason, many people have a difficult time with adverbs – but don't worry! They are really quite simple. Adverbs are similar to adjectives in that they provide more information; however, they describe verbs, adjectives, and even other adverbs. They do **not** describe nouns – that's an adjective's job.

Take the sentence: "The doctor said she hired a new employee."

It would give more information to say: "The doctor said she **recently** hired a new employee." Now we know more about *how* the action was executed. Adverbs typically describe when or how something has happened, how it looks, how it feels, etc.

Good vs. Well

A very common mistake that people make concerning adverbs is the misuse of the word "good."

"Good" is an adjective – things taste good, look good, and smell good. "Good" can even be a noun – "Superman does good" – when the word is speaking about "good" vs. "evil." HOWEVER, "good" is never an adverb.

People commonly say things like, "I did really good on that test," or, "I'm good." Ugh! This is NOT the correct way to speak! In those sentences, the word "good" is being used to describe an action: how a person **did**, or how a person **is**. Therefore, the adverb "well" should be used. "I did really **well** on that test." "I'm **well**."

The correct use of "well" and "good" can make or break a person's impression of your grammar – make sure to always speak correctly!

Study Tips for Improving Vocabulary and Grammar

1. You're probably pretty computer savvy and know the Internet very well. Visit the Online Writing Lab website, which is sponsored by Purdue University, at http://owl.english.purdue.edu. This site provides you with an excellent overview of syntax, writing style, and strategy. It also has helpful and lengthy review sections that include multiple-choice "Test Your Knowledge" quizzes, which provide immediate answers to the questions.

2. It's beneficial to read the entire passage first to determine its intended meaning BEFORE you attempt to answer any questions. Doing so provides you with key insight into a passage's syntax (especially verb tense, subject-verb agreement, modifier placement, writing style, and punctuation).

3. When you answer a question, use the "Process-of-Elimination Method" to determine the best answer. Try each of the four answers and determine which one BEST fits with the meaning of the paragraph. Find the BEST answer. Chances are that the BEST answer is the CORRECT answer.

Directions:

This test consists of four passages. In each passage, certain words and phrases have been underlined and numbered. The questions on each passage consist of alternatives for these underlined segments. Choose the alternative that follows standard written English, most accurately reflects the style and tone of the passage, or best relays the idea of the passage. Choose "No Change" if no change is necessary.

You are to choose the best answer to the question.

You will also find questions about a section of the passage, or the passage as a whole. These questions do not refer to the underlined portions of the passage, but are identified by a boxed number. For each question, choose the alternative that best answers the question.

PASSAGE I: Examining my Ecological Footprint

Examining the impact my lifestyle has on the earth's resources is a fascinating and
valuable thing to do. According to the Earth
Day Network ecological footprint calculator
created by the Sierra Club, it would take four
planet earths to sustain the human population if
everyone used as many resources as I do. My
"ecological footprint," or the amount of productive
area of the earth that is required to produce the
resources I consume, must then be much larger
2

like those of most of the population.
3
It is hard to balance the luxuries and opportunities I

have available to me: with doing what I know to be
4
better from an ecological standpoint.

One's ecological footprint is measured with
5
accounting for different factors such as how often
and how far one drives and travels by air, what kind
of structure one lives in, and what kind of goods one
consumes (and how far those consumer goods travel

1.
a) NO CHANGE
b) a fascinating or valuable thing to do.
c) fascinating to do and also valuable to do.
d) done to be fascinating or valuable.

2.
f) NO CHANGE
g) would have been
h) much
j) was much

3.
a) NO CHANGE
b) than those of
c) than footprints of
d) as the footprints of

4.
f) NO CHANGE
g) me, with
h) me; with
j) me with

5.
a) NO CHANGE
b) measured by
c) measured with
d) measured of

39

across the globe). For example, a person who lives in a freestanding home, which uses more energy to heat and cool than an apartment in a building does; who travels internationally several times per year; and who eats exotic, out-of-season foods which must be shipped in from other countries, rather than locally grown and raised food <u>which is</u> in season,
6
would have a large ecological footprint.

|7|

Although I get points for recycling, <u>my use of</u> public transportation, and living in an
8
apartment complex rather than a free-standing residence; my footprint expands when it is taken into account my not-entirely-local diet, my occasional use of a car, my three magazine subscriptions, and my history of flying more than ten hours a year. These are all examples of things that use a large amount of resources.

|9|

6.
   f) NO CHANGE
   g) that are
   h) those are
   j) which are

7. The last sentence in the above paragraph could be improved by:

   a) Being broken into short sentences.
   b) Being moved to the beginning of the paragraph.
   c) Including information about how the footprint is calculated.
   d) Taking out "for example" at the beginning of the sentence.

8.
   f) NO CHANGE
   g) use of
   h) using
   j) my using

9. The writer wants to add a sentence to the end of the paragraph that encourages others to calculate their own ecological footprint. Which of the following sentences would best accomplish this?

   a) There are many different ways that we use resources that may be surprising.
   b) Other things I do that use high amounts of resources include using a dryer for my laundry and leaving appliances plugged in when I'm out of the house.
   c) Sources of waste are often surprising; you can calculate your own ecological footprint online at myfootprint.org.

This examination of the impact my lifestyle <u>has</u>

<u>on the earth's resources</u> is fascinating and valuable
10
to me. It is fairly easy for me to recycle, so I do it,

but it would be much harder to <u>forgoing</u> the
11
opportunity to travel by plane or eat my favorite

<u>fruits; that</u> have been flown to the supermarket from
12
a different country. I feel that realizing just how

unfair my share of the <u>earths' resources has</u> been
13
should help me to change at least some of my bad

habit. Perhaps if we were all made aware of the true

cost of our habits, actions, and <u>choices, people</u>
14
would be more likely to take steps to reduce <u>his or</u>
15
<u>her</u> consumption of the earth's resources.

d) Sometimes the best way to reduce one's use of resources is to travel less.

10.
   f) NO CHANGE
   g) on the resources of the planet
   h) had on the earth's resources
   j) has on the earth resources

11.
   a) NO CHANGE
   b) forgo
   c) have forgone
   d) not forgo

12.
   f) NO CHANGE
   g) fruits, that
   h) fruits that
   j) fruits: that

13.
   a) NO CHANGE
   b) earth's resources has
   c) earths' resources have
   d) earth's resources have

14.
   f) NO CHANGE
   g) choices. People
   h) choices; people
   j) than people

15.
   a) NO CHANGE
   b) our
   c) their
   d) one's

PASSAGE II
The Sculptor Augusta Savage

Augusta <u>Savage were</u> a world-famous African-
        16
American sculptor. <u>Born in Florida,</u> her first formal
                          17
art training was in New York City at Cooper Union,

the school recommended to her by Solon Gorglum.

<u>While she studied,</u> she supported herself by doing
        18
odd jobs, including clerking and working in

laundries. In 1926 she exhibited her work at the

Sesquicentennial Exposition in Philadelphia. That

same year she was awarded a scholarship to study in

Rome. However, she was unable to accept the

award because she could not raise the money <u>she

would have needed</u> to live there.
        19

When she returned to the United States, she

exhibited her work at several important galleries. <u>In

addition to her own work,</u> Augusta Savage taught
        20
art classes in Harlem. During the Depression, she

helped African- American artists to enroll in the

Works Progress Administration arts project.

Throughout her career, she was an active

spokesperson for African-American artists in the

United <u>States. She also</u> was one of the principal

16.
  f) NO CHANGE
  g) Savage, was
  h) Savage, were
  j) Savage was

17.
  a) NO CHANGE
  b) She was born in Florida,
  c) While being born inFlorida,
  d) Although she was born in
       Florida,

18.
  f) NO CHANGE
  g) While she studied
  h) After studying
  j) She studied while

19.
  a) NO CHANGE
  b) she would need
  c) she needed
  d) she needs

20.
  f) NO CHANGE
  g) Additional to creating her own
       work,
  h) Additionally to her own work,
  j) In addition to creating her own
       work,

21
organizers of the Harlem Artists Guild.

In 1923 Savage, applied for a summer art
   22
program sponsored by the French government;

despite being more than qualified, she was turned

down by the international judging committee, solely

because of her race. Savage was deeply upset,

questioning the committee, beginning the first of
23

many public fights for equal rights in her life. The

incident got press coverage on both sides of the

Atlantic, and eventually the sole supportive

committee member, sculptor Hermon Atkins

MacNeil—who at one time had shared a studio with

Henry Ossawa Tanner—invited her to study with
                                    24
him.

She later cite him as one of her teachers.
                25

 In 1939, Augusta Savage received a

commission from the World's Fair and created a 16

foot tall plaster sculpture called *Lift Ev'ry Voice*

and Sing. Savage did not have any funds for a

bronze cast, or even to move and store it, and it was
                                              26

destroyed by bulldozers at the close of the fair.

However, small metal and plaster souvenir copies of

21. The author wants to combine the last two sentences of this paragraph. What is the best way to rewrite the underlined portion?

   a) States; she also
   b) States, although she also
   c) States, and also
   d) States and she

22.
   f) NO CHANGE
   g) 1923 Savage
   h) 1923, Savage
   j) 1923; Savage

23.
   a) NO CHANGE
   b) and questioned
   c) and questioning
   d) and so she questioned

24.
   f) NO CHANGE
   g) invited her to study with himself
   h) invited him to study with her
   j) gave her an invitation to study with him

25.
   a) NO CHANGE
   b) was citing
   c) citing
   d) cited

26.
   f) NO CHANGE
   g) the plaster
   h) them
   j) her

the sculpture <u>has</u> survived.
27

28

Perhaps Savage's more indelible legacy is the work of the students whom she taught in her studio, the Savage Studio of Arts and Crafts. Her students included Jacob Lawrence, Norman Lewis, and Gwendolyn Knight. Lawrence was a Cubist painter whose work is hosted in museums across the country. Lewis was an Abstract Expressionist painter who often dealt with music and jazz in abstract ways. <u>Knight who was born in Barbados</u>
29
founded an organization to support young artists. Augusta Savage <u>worked tireless</u> to teach these
30
artists, help them to secure funding, and support their careers.

27.
   a) NO CHANGE
   b) have
   c) were
   d) would

28. Which sentence would best fit at the beginning of the paragraph that now begins "In 1939"?

   f) Her education in the arts was substantial after working with so many high profit sculptors.
   g) African-Americans were still facing terrible discrimination at the end of the 1930's.
   h) The World's Fair is a huge art exhibit that occurs every two to four years.
   j) Throughout the 1930's, her profile as an artist continued to grow.

29.
   a) NO CHANGE
   b) Knight, who was born in Barbados
   c) Knight who was born in Barbados,
   d) Knight, who was born in Barbados,

30.
   f) NO CHANGE
   g) worked tirelessly
   h) worked herself tireless
   j) was working tireless

PASSAGE III
History of Art for Beginners and Students – Ancient Painting

The following passage is adapted from Clara Erskine Clément's History of Art for Beginners and Students, first published in 1887 (public domain; errors inserted for the purposes of crafting questions).

In speaking of art we often contrast the useful or mechanical arts with the Fine Arts; by these terms we denote the difference between the arts which are used in making such things as are necessary and useful in civilized life, and the arts by which ornamental and beautiful things made. The fine
31
arts are Architecture, Sculpture, Painting, Poetry, and Music, and though we could live if none of these existed, yet life would be far from the pleasant
32
experience that it is often made to be through the
33
enjoyment of these arts.

Of course, forms of art can be both fine and useful. While painting belongs to the fine or beautiful arts, it is a very useful art in many ways. For example, when a school-book is illustrated, how much more easily we understand the subject we are studying through the help we get from pictures of objects or places that we have not otherwise seen. Pictures of natural scenery bring all countries before our eyes in such a way that by looking at it, while
34

31.
a) NO CHANGE
b) things.
c) things are made.
d) things are used.

32.
f) NO CHANGE
g) existed,
h) yet,
j) existed and yet

33.
a) NO CHANGE
b) made out to be
c) made
d) is

34.
f) NO CHANGE
g) those
h) them
j) one

45

reading books of travel, we may know a great deal

more about lands we have never seen, and may

never be able to visit.

[35]

St. Augustine, who wrote in the fourth <u>century,</u>
36
<u>says</u> that "pictures are the books of the simple or

unlearned." This is just as true now as then, and we

should regard pictures as one of the best methods

for teaching. The cultivation of the

imagination is very <u>important because for</u> this way
37
we can add much to our individual happiness. Thus

one of the uses of pictures is that they give us a

clear idea of what we have not seen; a second use is

that they <u>are exciting to</u> our imaginations, and often
38
help us to forget disagreeable circumstances and

unpleasant surroundings. Through this power, if we

are in a dark, narrow street, in a house which is not

to our liking, <u>or in the midst of any unpleasant</u>
39
<u>happenings</u>, we are able to fix our thoughts upon a

photograph or picture that may be there, and

we are able to imagine ourselves far, far

away, in some spot where nature makes everything

pleasant and soothes us into forgetfulness of all that

makes us unhappy. Many an invalid—many

an unfortunate person is made content by pictures

35. Which of the following sentences could be added to the above paragraph to give another example of how pictures are useful as well as decorative?

   a) Pictures are not useful, however, when they distract students from the purpose of a text.
   b) Pictures can be a beautiful addition to our homes.
   c) Doctors often use pictures when studying the body to help them learn organs and systems.
   d) This is helpful because people really don't travel to other lands anymore.

36.
   f) NO CHANGE
   g) century says
   h) century said
   j) century, said

37.
   a) NO CHANGE
   b) important, because in
   c) important, because for
   d) important; in

38.
   f) NO CHANGE
   g) exciting
   h) excite
   j) excited

39. If the writer deletes this section of this sentence, what will be lost?

   a) Nothing; the meaning of the sentence will not change.
   b) The argument that pictures are useful.
   c) The example of pictures being educational.
   d) The generalization of the specific example to all unpleasant circumstances.

during hours that would <u>otherwise be</u> wretched.
40

This is the result of cultivating the <u>imagination and</u>

<u>when</u> this is done, we have a source of pleasure
41

within ourselves which can never be taken from

us.

It often happens that we see two people <u>doing</u>
42

the same work and are situated in the same way in

the world, but who are different in their <u>manner</u>
43

<u>one</u> is light-hearted and happy, the other sullen and

sad. If you can find out the truth, it will be that

the sad one is matter-of-fact, and has no

imagination—he can only think of his work and

what concerns him personally; but the merry one

would surprise you if you could read his thoughts—

if you could know the distances <u>they have</u> passed
44

over, and what a vast difference there is between his

thought and his work. So while it is natural for

almost everyone to exclaim <u>joyful</u> at the beauty of
45

pictures, and to enjoy looking at them simply, I

wish my readers to think of their uses also, and

understand the benefits that may be derived from

them.

40.

f) NO CHANGE
g) tend to be
h) however be
j) be

41.

a) NO CHANGE
b) imagination so when
c) imagination, and when
d) imagination; when

42.

f) NO CHANGE
g) are doing
h) who do
j) done

43.

a) NO CHANGE
b) manner; one
c) manner. One
d) manner: one

44.

f) NO CHANGE
g) he has
h) it has
j) you have

45.

a) NO CHANGE
b) joyfully
c) joy
d) with joy

1. a)

2. f)

3. b)

4. j)

5. b)

6. f)

7. a)

8. **h)** This is an instance of parallelism, where you want verbs in a list in a sentence to have the same form.

9. c)

10. f)

11. b)

12. h)

13. b)

14. f)

15. c)

16. j)

17. **d)** This is an example of a misplaced modifier and needs to be edited.

18. f)

19. a)

20. j)

21. c)

22. h)

23. b)

24. f)

25. d)

26. g)

27. b)

28. **j)** This sentence best follows the topic of the passage while leading into the new information in this paragraph.

29. d)

30. g)

31. c)

32. g)

33. d)

34. h)

35. c)

36. f)

37. b)

38. h)

39. d)

40. f)

41. c)

42. h)

43. d)

44. f)

45. b)

Chapter 3: Math

Before we begin our review, remember that there is no wrong-answer penalty on this exam, so try not to leave an answer selection blank. Of course, since the objective is to get as many right answers as possible, always use the process of elimination before choosing your answer. While the amount of time allotted for this section may seem like too little for the amount of questions, many of the questions are designed to be simpler than others. We recommend going through the exam first, quickly answering those questions which seem easier than others. Then, on your second run-through, focus your attention on the more-complicated problems.

The Most Common Mistakes

People make mistakes all the time – but during a test, those mistakes can cost you a passing score. Watch out for these common mistakes that people make on the PARAPRO:

- Answering with the wrong sign (positive / negative).

- Mixing up the Order of Operations.

- Misplacing a decimal.

- Not reading the question thoroughly (and therefore providing an answer that was not asked for.)

- Circling the wrong letter, or filling in wrong circle choice.

If you're thinking, "Those ideas are just common sense" – exactly! Most of the mistakes made on the PARAPRO are simple mistakes. Regardless, they still result in a wrong answer and the loss of a potential point.

Helpful Strategies

- **Go Back to the Basics**: First and foremost, practice your basic skills: sign changes, order of operations, simplifying fractions, and equation manipulation. These are the skills used most on the test, though they are applied in different contexts. Remember that when it comes right down to it, all math problems rely on the four basic skills of addition, subtraction, multiplication, and division. All that changes is the order in which they are used to solve a problem.

- **Don't Rely on Mental Math**: Using mental math is great for eliminating answer choices, but ALWAYS WRITE IT DOWN! This cannot be stressed enough. Use whatever paper is provided; by writing and/or drawing out the problem, you are more likely to catch any mistakes. The act of writing things down forces you to organize your calculations, leading to an improvement in your score.

- **The Three-Times Rule**:

  1. **Step One – Read the question**: Write out the given information.

  2. **Step Two – Read the question**: Set up your equation(s) and solve.

  3. **Step Three – Read the question:** Make sure that your answer makes sense (is the amount too large or small, is the answer in the correct unit of measure, etc.).

- **Make an Educated Guess**: Eliminate those answer choices which you are relatively sure are incorrect, and then guess from the remaining choices. Educated guessing is critical to increasing your score.

Calculators

Calculators may only be used on the mathematics section, but all the questions can be answered without one. Any four-function, graphing or scientific calculator may be used, unless it has the following prohibited features.

As stated before, you may **NOT** use a calculator with the following functions:

- Calculators with built-in computer algebra systems.

- Texas Instruments: TI – 89, TI – 92.

- Hewlett-Packard: hp 48GII, and all models beginning with hp 40G, hp 49G, or hp50G.

- Casio: Algebra fx 2.0, ClassPad 300, and all models beginning with CFX-9970G.

- Pocket organizers.

- Handheld or laptop computers.

- Electronic writing pads or pen-input devices.

- Calculators with a typewriter keypad (QWERTY).

- Calculators built into cell phones or other electronic devices.

Math Concepts Tested on the PARAPRO

You need to practice in order to score well on the test. To make the most out of your practice, use this guide to determine the areas for which you need more review. Most importantly, practice all areas under testing circumstances (a quiet area, a timed practice test, no looking up facts as you practice, etc.)

When reviewing, take your time and let your brain recall the necessary math. If you are taking this test, then you have already had course instruction in these areas. The examples given will "jog" your memory.

The next few pages will cover various math subjects (starting with the basics, but in no particular order), along with worked examples.

Numbers and Operations
Positive and Negative Number Rules

Adding, multiplying, and dividing numbers can yield positive or negative values depending on the signs of the original numbers. Knowing these rules can help determine if your answer is correct.

$(+) + (-) =$ the sign of the larger number
$(-) + (-) =$ negative number
$(-) \times (-) =$ positive number
$(-) \times (+) =$ negative number
$(-) \div (-) =$ positive number
$(-) \div (+) =$ negative number

Examples
1.   Find the product of -10 and 47.
$(-) \times (+) = (-)$
$-10 \times 47 = -470$

2.   What is the sum of -65 and -32?
$(-) + (-) = (-)$
$-65 + -32 = -97$

3.   Is the product of -7 and 4 less than -7, between -7 and 4, or greater than 4?
$(-) \times (+) = (-)$
$-7 \times 4 = -28$, which is less than -7

51

4. What is the value of −16 divided by 2.5?

$(-) \div (+) = (-)$

$-16 \div 2.5 = \mathbf{-6.4}$

Order of Operations

Operations in a mathematical expression are always performed in a specific order, which is described by the acronym PEMDAS:

    1. Parentheses
    2. Exponents
    3. Multiplication
    4. Division
    5. Addition
    6. Subtraction

Perform the operations within parentheses first, and then address any exponents. After those steps, perform all multiplication and division. These are carried out from left to right as they appear in the problem. Finally, do all required addition and subtraction, also from left to right as each operation appears in the problem.

Examples

1. Solve: $[-(2)^2 - (4 + 7)]$

First, complete operations within parentheses:

$-(2)^2 - (11)$

Second, calculate the value of exponential numbers:

$-(4) - (11)$

Finally, do addition and subtraction:

$-4 - 11 = \mathbf{-15}$

2.   Solve: $(5)^2 \div 5 + 4 \times 2$
First, calculate the value of exponential numbers:
$(25) \div 5 + 4 \times 2$
Second, calculate division and multiplication from left to right:
$5 + 8$
Finally, do addition and subtraction:
$5 + 8 = \textbf{13}$

3.   Solve the expression: $15 \times (4 + 8) - 3^3$
First, complete operations within parentheses:
$15 \times (12) - 3^3$
Second, calculate the value of exponential numbers:
$15 \times (12) - 27$
Third, calculate division and multiplication from left to right:
$180 - 27$
Finally, do addition and subtraction from left to right:
$180 - 27 = \textbf{153}$

4.   Solve the expression: $(\frac{5}{2} \times 4) + 23 - 4^2$
First, complete operations within parentheses:
$(10) + 23 - 4^2$
Second, calculate the value of exponential numbers:
$(10) + 23 - 16$
Finally, do addition and subtraction from left to right:
$(10) + 23 - 16$
$33 - 16 = \textbf{17}$

Greatest Common Factor

The greatest common factor (GCF) of a set of numbers is the largest number that can evenly divide into all of the numbers in the set. To find the GCF of a set, find all of the factors of each number in the set. A factor is a whole number that can be multiplied by another whole number to result in the original number. For example, the number 10 has four factors: 1, 2, 5, and 10. (When listing the factors of a number, remember to include 1 and the number itself.) The largest number that is a factor for each number in the set is the GCF.

Examples
1.   Find the greatest common factor of 24 and 18.
Factors of 24: 1, 2, 3, 4, 6, 8, 12, 24
Factors of 18: 1, 2, 3, 6, 9, 18
The greatest common factor is 6.

2.   Find the greatest common factor of 121 and 44.
Since these numbers are larger, it's easier to start with the smaller number when listing factors.
Factors of 44: 1, 2, 4, 11, 22, 44
Now, it's not necessary to list all of the factors of 121. Instead, we can eliminate those factors of 44 which do not divide evenly into 121:

121 is not evenly divisible by 2, 4, 22, or 44 because it is an odd number. This leaves only 1 and 11 as common factors, so the **GCF is 11**.

3.   First aid kits are being assembled at a summer camp. A complete first aid kit requires bandages, sutures, and sterilizing swabs, and each of the kits must be identical to other kits. If the camp's total supplies include 52 bandages, 13 sutures, and 39 sterilizing swabs, how many complete first aid kits can be assembled without having any leftover materials?

This problem is asking for the greatest common factor of 52, 13, and 39. The first step is to find all of the factors of the smallest number, 13.

Factors of 13: 1, 13

13 is a prime number, meaning that its only factors are 1 and itself. Next, we check to see if 13 is also a factor of 39 and 52:

$13 \times 2 = 26$

$13 \times 3 = 39$

$13 \times 4 = 52$

We can see that 39 and 52 are both multiples of 13. This means that **13 first aid kits can be made without having any leftover materials.**

4.   Elena is making sundaes for her friends. She has 20 scoops of chocolate ice cream and 16 scoops of strawberry. If she wants to make identical sundaes and use all of her ice cream, how many sundaes can she make?

Arranging things into identical groups with no leftovers is always a tip that the problem calls for finding the greatest common factor. To find the GCF of 16 and 20, the first step is to factor both numbers:

Factors of 16: 1, 2, 4, 8, 16

Factors of 20: 1, 2, 4, 5, 10, 20

From these lists, we see that **4 is the GCF**. Elena can make 4 sundaes, each with 5 scoops of chocolate ice cream and 4 scoops of strawberry. Any other combination would result in leftover ice cream or sundaes that are not identical.

Comparison of Rational Numbers

Number comparison problems present numbers in different formats and ask which is larger or smaller, or whether the numbers are equivalent. The important step in solving these problems is to convert the numbers to the same format so that it is easier to see how they compare. If numbers are given in the same format, or after they have been converted, determine which number is smaller or if the numbers are equal. Remember that for negative numbers, higher numbers are actually smaller.

Examples

1.   Is $4\frac{3}{4}$ greater than, equal to, or less than $\frac{18}{4}$?

These numbers are in different formats—one is a mixed fraction and the other is just a fraction. So, the first step is to convert the mixed fraction to a fraction:

$$4\frac{3}{4} = \frac{4 \times 4 + 3}{4} = \frac{19}{4}$$

Once the mixed number is converted, it is easier to see that $\frac{19}{4}$ is greater than $\frac{18}{4}$.

2.   Which of the following numbers has the greatest value: 104.56, 104.5, or 104.6?

These numbers are already in the same format, so the decimal values just need to be compared. Remember that zeros can be added after the decimal without changing the value, so the three numbers can be rewritten as:

104.56

104.50

104.60

From this list, it is clearer to see that **104.60 is the greatest** because 0.60 is larger than 0.50 and 0.56.

3.   Is 65% greater than, less than, or equal to $\frac{13}{20}$?

The first step is to convert the numbers into the same format. 65% is the same as $\frac{65}{100}$.

Next, the fractions need to be converted to have the same denominator. It is difficult to compare fractions with different denominators. Using a factor of $\frac{5}{5}$ on the second fraction will give common denominators:

$$\frac{13}{20} \times \frac{5}{5} = \frac{65}{100}$$

Now, it is easy to see that **the numbers are equivalent**.

Units of Measurement

You are expected to memorize some units of measurement. These are given below. When doing unit conversion problems (i.e., when converting one unit to another), find the conversion factor, then apply that factor to the given measurement to find the new units.

UNIT PREFIXES

Prefix	Symbol	Multiplication Factor
tera	T	1,000,000,000,000
giga	G	1,000,000,000
mega	M	1,000,000
kilo	k	1,000
hecto	h	100
deca	da	10
base unit	--	--
deci	d	0.1
centi	c	0.01
milli	m	0.001
micro	μ	0.0000001
nano	n	0.0000000001
pico	p	0.0000000000001

UNITS AND CONVERSION FACTORS

Dimension	American	SI
length	inch/foot/yard/mile	meter
mass	ounce/pound/ton	gram
volume	cup/pint/quart/gallon	liter
force	pound-force	newton
pressure	pound-force per square inch	pascal
work and energy	cal/British thermal unit	joule
temperature	Fahrenheit	kelvin
charge	faraday	coulomb

Conversion Factors

1 in. = 2.54 cm 1 yd. = 0.914 m 1 mi. = 1.61 km 1 gal. = 3.785 L 1 oz. = 28.35 g	1 lb. = 0.454 kg 1 cal = 4.19 J $1°F = \frac{5}{9}(°F - 32°C)$ 1 cm^3 = 1 mL 1 hr = 3600 s

Examples

1.   A fence measures 15 ft. long. How many yards long is the fence?

1 yd. = 3 ft.

$\frac{15}{3}$ = **5 yd.**

2.   A pitcher can hold 24 cups. How many gallons can it hold?

1 gal. = 16 cups

$\frac{24}{16}$ = **1.5 gallons**

3.   A spool of wire holds 144 in. of wire. If Mario has 3 spools, how many feet of wire does he have?

12 in. = 1 ft.

$\frac{144}{12}$ = 12 ft.

12 ft. × 3 spools = **36 ft. of wire**

4.   A ball rolling across a table travels 6 inches per second. How many feet will it travel in 1 minute? This problem can be worked in two steps: finding how many inches are covered in 1 minute, and then converting that value to feet. It can also be worked the opposite way, by finding how many feet it travels in 1 second and then converting that to feet traveled per minute. The first method is shown below.

1 min. = 60 sec.

(6 in.)/(sec.) × 60 s = 360 in.

1 ft. = 12 in.

(360 in.)/(12 in.) = **30 ft.**

5.   How many millimeters are in 0.5 m?

1 meter = 1000 mm

0.5 meters = **500 mm**

6.   A lead ball weighs 38 g. How many kilograms does it weigh?

1 kg = 1000 g

$\dfrac{38}{1000}$ g = **0.038 kg**

7.   How many cubic centimeters are in 10 L?

1 L = 1000 ml

10 L = 1000 ml × 10

10 L = **10,000 ml or cm^3**

8.   Jennifer's pencil was initially 10 centimeters long. After she sharpened it, it was 9.6 centimeters long. How many millimeters did she lose from her pencil by sharpening it?

1 cm = 10 mm

10 cm − 9.6 cm = 0.4 cm lost

0.4 cm = 10 × .4 mm = **4 mm were lost**

Decimals and Fractions

Adding and Subtracting Decimals

When adding and subtracting decimals, line up the numbers so that the decimals are aligned. You want to subtract the ones place from the ones place, the tenths place from the tenths place, etc.

Examples

1.   Find the sum of 17.07 and 2.52.

```
 17.07
+2.52
 19.59
```

2.   Jeannette has 7.4 gallons of gas in her tank. After driving, she has 6.8 gallons. How many gallons of gas did she use?

```
  7.4
− 6.8
  0.6 gal
```

Multiplying and Dividing Decimals

When multiplying decimals, start by multiplying the numbers normally. You can then determine the placement of the decimal point in the result by adding the number of digits after the decimal in each of the numbers you multiplied together.

When dividing decimals, you should move the decimal point in the divisor (the number you're dividing by) until it is a whole. You can then move the decimal in the dividend (the number you're dividing into) the same number of places in the same direction. Finally, divide the new numbers normally to get the correct answer.

Examples

1.   What is the product of 0.25 and 1.4?

$25 \times 14 = 350$

There are 2 digits after the decimal in 0.25 and one digit after the decimal in 1.4. Therefore the product should have 3 digits after the decimal: **0.350** is the correct answer.

2.   Find 0.8 ÷ 0.2.

Change 0.2 to 2 by moving the decimal one space to the right.

Next, move the decimal one space to the right on the dividend. 0.8 becomes 8.

Now, divide 8 by 2. $8 \div 2 = 4$

3.   Find the quotient when 40 is divided by 0.25.

First, change the divisor to a whole number: 0.25 becomes 25.

Next, change the dividend to match the divisor by moving the decimal two spaces to the right, so 40 becomes 4000.

Now divide: $4000 \div 25 = \mathbf{160}$

Working with Fractions

FRACTIONS are made up of two parts: the **NUMERATOR**, which appears above the bar, and the **DENOMINATOR**, which is below it. If a fraction is in its **SIMPLEST FORM**, the numerator and the denominator share no common factors. A fraction with a numerator larger than its denominator is an **IMPROPER FRACTION**; when the denominator is larger, it's a **PROPER FRACTION**.

Improper fractions can be converted into proper fractions by dividing the numerator by the denominator. The resulting whole number is placed to the left of the fraction, and the remainder becomes the new numerator; the denominator does not change. The new number is called a **MIXED NUMBER** because it contains a whole number and a fraction. Mixed numbers can be turned into improper fractions through the reverse process: multiply the whole number by the denominator and add the numerator to get the new numerator.

Examples

1.   Simplify the fraction $\frac{121}{77}$.

121 and 77 share a common factor of 11. So, if we divide each by 11 we can simplify the fraction:

$$\frac{121}{77} = \frac{11}{11} \times \frac{11}{7} = \mathbf{\frac{11}{7}}$$

2.   Convert $\frac{37}{5}$ into a proper fraction.

Start by dividing the numerator by the denominator:

$37 \div 5 = 7$ with a remainder of 2

Now build a mixed number with the whole number and the new numerator:

$$\frac{37}{5} = \mathbf{7\frac{2}{5}}$$

Multiplying and Dividing Fractions

To multiply fractions, convert any mixed numbers into improper fractions and multiply the numerators together and the denominators together. Reduce to lowest terms if needed.

To divide fractions, first convert any mixed fractions into single fractions. Then, invert the second fraction so that the denominator and numerator are switched. Finally, multiply the numerators together and the denominators together.

Examples

1.   What is the product of $\frac{1}{12}$ and $\frac{6}{8}$?

Simply multiply the numerators together and the denominators together, then reduce:

$$\frac{1}{12} \times \frac{6}{8} = \frac{6}{96} = \mathbf{\frac{1}{16}}$$

Sometimes it's easier to reduce fractions before multiplying if you can:

$$\frac{1}{12} \times \frac{6}{8} = \frac{1}{12} \times \frac{3}{4} = \frac{3}{48} \ \mathbf{\frac{1}{16}}$$

2.   Find $\frac{7}{8} \div \frac{1}{4}$.

For a fraction division problem, invert the second fraction and then multiply and reduce:

$$\frac{7}{8} \div \frac{1}{4} = \frac{7}{8} \times \frac{4}{1} = \frac{28}{8} = \mathbf{\frac{7}{2}}$$

3. What is the quotient of $\frac{2}{5} \div 1\frac{1}{5}$?

This is a fraction division problem, so the first step is to convert the mixed number to an improper fraction:

$1\frac{1}{5} = \frac{5 \times 1 + 1}{5} = \frac{6}{5}$

Now, divide the fractions. Remember to invert the second fraction, and then multiply normally:

$\frac{2}{5} \div \frac{6}{5} = \frac{2}{5} \times \frac{5}{6} = \frac{10}{30} = \frac{1}{3}$

4. A recipe calls for $\frac{1}{4}$ cup of sugar. If 8.5 batches of the recipe are needed, how many cups of sugar will be used?

This is a fraction multiplication problem: $\frac{1}{4} \times 8\frac{1}{2}$.

First, we need to convert the mixed number into a proper fraction:

$8\frac{1}{2} = \frac{8 \times 2 + 1}{2} = \frac{17}{2}$

Now, multiply the fractions across the numerators and denominators, and then reduce:

$\frac{1}{4} \times 8\frac{1}{2} = \frac{1}{4} \times \frac{17}{2} = \frac{17}{8}$ **cups of sugar**

Adding and Subtracting Fractions

Adding and subtracting fractions requires a **COMMON DENOMINATOR**. To find the common denominator, you can multiply each fraction by the number 1. With fractions, any number over itself (e.g., $\frac{5}{5}$, $\frac{12}{12}$, etc.) is equivalent to 1, so multiplying by such a fraction can change the denominator without changing the value of the fraction. Once the denominators are the same, the numerators can be added or subtracted.

To add mixed numbers, you can first add the whole numbers and then the fractions. To subtract mixed numbers, convert each number to an improper fraction, then subtract the numerators.

Examples

1. Simplify the expression $\frac{2}{3} - \frac{1}{5}$.

First, multiply each fraction by a factor of 1 to get a common denominator. How do you know which factor of 1 to use? Look at the other fraction and use the number found in that denominator:

$\frac{2}{3} - \frac{1}{5} = \frac{2}{3}\left(\frac{5}{5}\right) - \frac{1}{5}\left(\frac{3}{3}\right) = \frac{10}{15} - \frac{3}{15}$

Once the fractions have a common denominator, simply subtract the numerators:

$\frac{10}{15} - \frac{3}{15} = \frac{7}{15}$

2. Find $2\frac{1}{3} - \frac{3}{2}$.

This is a fraction subtraction problem with a mixed number, so the first step is to convert the mixed number to an improper fraction:

$2\frac{1}{3} = \frac{2 \times 3 + 1}{3} = \frac{7}{3}$

Next, convert each fraction so they share a common denominator:

$\frac{7}{3} \times \frac{2}{2} = \frac{14}{6}$

$\frac{3}{2} \times \frac{3}{3} = \frac{9}{6}$

Now, subtract the fractions by subtracting the numerators:

$\frac{14}{6} - \frac{9}{6} = \frac{5}{6}$

3. Find the sum of $\frac{9}{16}$, $\frac{1}{2}$, and $\frac{7}{4}$.

For this fraction addition problem, we need to find a common denominator. Notice that 2 and 4 are both factors of 16, so 16 can be the common denominator:

$$\frac{1}{2} \times \frac{8}{8} = \frac{8}{16}$$

$$\frac{7}{4} \times \frac{4}{4} = \frac{28}{16}$$

$$\frac{9}{16} + \frac{8}{16} + \frac{28}{16} = \mathbf{\frac{45}{16}}$$

4. Sabrina has $\frac{2}{3}$ of a can of red paint. Her friend Amos has $\frac{1}{6}$ of a can. How much red paint do they have combined?

To add fractions, make sure that they have a common denominator. Since 3 is a factor of 6, 6 can be the common denominator:

$$\frac{2}{3} \times \frac{2}{2} = \frac{4}{6}$$

Now, add the numerators:

$$\frac{4}{6} + \frac{1}{6} = \mathbf{\frac{5}{6} \text{ of a can}}$$

Converting Fractions to Decimals

Calculators are not allowed on the PARAPRO, which can make handling fractions and decimals intimidating for many test takers. However, there are several techniques you can use to help you convert between the two forms.

The first thing to do is simply memorize common decimals and their fractional equivalents; a list of these is given in Table 3.4. With these values, it's possible to convert more complicated fractions as well. For example, $\frac{2}{5}$ is just $\frac{1}{5}$ multiplied by 2, so $\frac{2}{5} = 0.2 \times 2 = 0.4$.

COMMON DECIMALS AND FRACTIONS	
fraction	decimal
$\frac{1}{2}$	0.5
$\frac{1}{3}$	$0.\overline{33}$
$\frac{1}{4}$	0.25
$\frac{1}{5}$	0.2
$\frac{1}{6}$	$0.1\overline{66}$
$\frac{1}{7}$	$0.\overline{142857}$
$\frac{1}{8}$	0.125

$\frac{1}{9}$	$0.\overline{11}$
$\frac{1}{10}$	0.1

Knowledge of common decimal equivalents to fractions can also help you estimate. This skill can be particularly helpful on multiple-choice tests like the PARAPRO, where excluding incorrect answers can be just as helpful as knowing how to find the right one. For example, to find $\frac{5}{8}$ in decimal form for an answer, you can eliminate any answers less than 0.5 because $\frac{4}{8} = 0.5$. You may also know that $\frac{6}{8}$ is the same as $\frac{3}{4}$ or 0.75, so anything above 0.75 can be eliminated as well.

Another helpful trick can be used if the denominator is easily divisible by 100: in the fraction $\frac{9}{20}$, you know 20 goes into 100 five times, so you can multiply the top and bottom by 5 to get $\frac{45}{100}$ or 0.45.

If none of these techniques work, you'll need to find the decimal by dividing the denominator by the numerator using long division.

Examples

1. Write $\frac{8}{18}$ as a decimal.

The first step here is to simplify the fraction:

$$\frac{8}{18} = \frac{4}{9}$$

Now it's clear that the fraction is a multiple of $\frac{1}{9}$, so you can easily find the decimal using a value you already know:

$$\frac{4}{9} = \frac{1}{9} \times 4 = 0.\overline{11} \times 4 = \mathbf{0.\overline{44}}$$

2. Write the fraction $\frac{3}{16}$ as a decimal.

None of the tricks above will work for this fraction, so you need to do long division:

The decimal will go in front of the answer, so now you know that $\frac{3}{16} = \mathbf{0.1875}$.

Converting Decimals to Fractions

Converting a decimal into a fraction is more straightforward than the reverse process is. To convert a decimal, simply use the numbers that come after the decimal as the numerator in the fraction. The denominator will be a power of 10 that matches the place value for the original decimal. For example, the numerator for 0.46 would be 100 because the last number is in the tenths place; likewise, the denominator for 0.657 would be 1000 because the last number is in the thousandths place. Once this fraction has been set up, all that's left is to simplify it.

Example

Convert 0.45 into a fraction.

The last number in the decimal is in the hundredths place, so we can easily set up a fraction:

$0.45 = \frac{45}{100}$

The next step is to simply reduce the fraction down to the lowest common denominator. Here, both 45 and 100 are divisible by 5: 45 divided by 5 is 9, and 100 divided by 5 is 20. Therefore, you're left with:

$\frac{45}{100} = \frac{9}{20}$

Ratios

A **RATIO** tells you how many of one thing exists in relation to the number of another thing. Unlike fractions, ratios do not give a part relative to a whole; instead, they compare two values. For example, if you have 3 apples and 4 oranges, the ratio of apples to oranges is 3 to 4. Ratios can be written using words (3 to 4), fractions $\left(\frac{3}{4}\right)$, or colons (3:4).

In order to work with ratios, it's helpful to rewrite them as a fraction expressing a part to a whole. For example, in the example above you have 7 total pieces of fruit, so the fraction of your fruit that are apples is $\frac{3}{7}$, and oranges make up $\frac{4}{7}$ of your fruit collection.

One last important thing to consider when working with ratios is the units of the values being compared. On the PARAPRO, you may be asked to rewrite a ratio using the same units on both sides. For example, you might have to rewrite the ratio 3 minutes to 7 seconds as 180 seconds to 7 seconds.

Examples

1.   There are 90 voters in a room, and each is either a Democrat or a Republican. The ratio of Democrats to Republicans is 5:4. How many Republicans are there?

We know that there are 5 Democrats for every 4 Republicans in the room, which means for every 9 people, 4 are Republicans.

$5 + 4 = 9$

Fraction of Democrats: $\frac{5}{9}$

Fraction of Republicans: $\frac{4}{9}$

If $\frac{4}{9}$ of the 90 voters are Republicans, then:

$\frac{4}{9}$ x 90 = **40 voters are Republicans**

2.   The ratio of students to teachers in a school is 15:1. If there are 38 teachers, how many students attend the school?

To solve this ratio problem, we can simply multiply both sides of the ratio by the desired value to find the number of students that correspond to having 38 teachers:

$\frac{15 \text{ students}}{1 \text{ teacher}} \times 38 \text{ teachers} = 570 \text{ students}$

The school has **570 students**.

Proportions

A **PROPORTION** is an equation which states that 2 ratios are equal. Proportions are usually written as 2 fractions joined by an equal sign $\left(\frac{a}{b} = \frac{c}{d}\right)$, but they can also be written using colons ($a : b :: c : d$). Note that in a proportion, the units must be the same in both numerators and in both denominators.

Often you will be given 3 of the values in a proportion and asked to find the 4th. In these types of problems, you can solve for the missing variable by cross-multiplying—multiply the numerator of each fraction by the denominator of the other to get an equation with no fractions as shown below. You can then solve the equation using basic algebra. (For more on solving basic equations, see *Algebraic Expressions and Equations*.)

$$\frac{a}{b} = \frac{c}{d} \rightarrow ad = bc$$

Examples

1. A train traveling 120 miles takes 3 hours to get to its destination. How long will it take for the train to travel 180 miles?

Start by setting up the proportion:

$$\frac{120 \text{ miles}}{3 \text{ hours}} = \frac{180 \text{ miles}}{x \text{ hours}}$$

Note that it doesn't matter which value is placed in the numerator or denominator, as long as it is the same on both sides. Now, solve for the missing quantity through cross–multiplication:

120 miles $\times$ x hours = 3 hours $\times$ 180 miles

Now solve the equation:

$$x = \frac{3 \text{ hours} \times 180 \text{ miles}}{120 \text{ miles}}$$

x = **4.5 hours**

2. One acre of wheat requires 500 gallons of water. How many acres can be watered with 2600 gallons?

Set up the equation:

$$\frac{1 \text{ acre}}{500 \text{ gal.}} = \frac{x \text{ acres}}{2600 \text{ gal.}}$$

Then solve for x:

$$x = \frac{1 \text{ acre} \times 2600 \text{ gal.}}{500 \text{ gal.}}$$

$$x = \frac{26}{5} \text{ or } \textbf{5.2 acres}$$

3. If $35 : 5 :: 49 : x$, find x.

This problem presents two equivalent ratios that can be set up in a fraction equation:

$$\frac{35}{5} = \frac{49}{x}$$

You can then cross-multiply to solve for x:

$$35x = 49 \times 5$$
$$x = 7$$

Percentages

A PERCENT is the ratio of a part to the whole. Questions may give the part and the whole and ask for the percent, or give the percent and the whole and ask for the part, or give the part and the percent and ask for the value of the whole. The equation for percentages can be rearranged to solve for any of these:

$$percent = \frac{part}{whole}$$
$$part = whole \times percent$$
$$whole = \frac{part}{percent}$$

In the equations above, the percent should always be expressed as a decimal. In order to convert a decimal into a percentage value, simply multiply it by 100. So, if you've read 5 pages (the part) of a 10-page article (the whole), you've read $\frac{5}{10}$ = 0.5 or 50%. (The percent sign (%) is used once the decimal has been multiplied by 100.)

Note that when solving these problems, the units for the part and the whole should be the same. If you're reading a book, saying you've read 5 pages out of 15 chapters doesn't make any sense.

Examples

1.   45 is 15% of what number?

Set up the appropriate equation and solve. Don't forget to change 15% to a decimal value:

$$whole = \frac{part}{percent} = \frac{45}{0.15} = \mathbf{300}$$

2.   Jim spent 30% of his paycheck at the fair. He spent $15 for a hat, $30 for a shirt, and $20 playing games. How much was his check? (Round to nearest dollar.)

Set up the appropriate equation and solve:

$$whole = \frac{part}{percent} = \frac{15+30+20}{0.30} = \mathbf{\$217.00}$$

3.   What percent of 65 is 39?

Set up the equation and solve:

$$percent = \frac{part}{whole} = \frac{39}{65} = \mathbf{0.6 \text{ or } 60\%}$$

4.   Greta and Max sell cable subscriptions. In a given month, Greta sells 45 subscriptions and Max sells 51. If 240 total subscriptions were sold in that month, what percent were not sold by Greta or Max?

You can use the information in the question to figure out what percentage of subscriptions were sold by Max and Greta:

$$percent = \frac{part}{whole} = \frac{51+45}{240} = \frac{96}{240} = 0.4 \text{ or } 40\%$$

However, the question asks how many subscriptions weren't sold by Max or Greta. If they sold 40%, then the other salespeople sold 100% − 40% = **60%**.

5.   Grant needs to score 75% on an exam. If the exam has 45 questions, at least how many does he need to answer correctly?

Set up the equation and solve. Remember to convert 75% to a decimal value:

$$part = whole \times percent = 45 \times 0.75 = 33.75\text{, so he needs to answer at least } \mathbf{34 \text{ questions correctly}}.$$

Percent Change

PERCENT CHANGE problems will ask you to calculate how much a given quantity changed. The problems are solved in a similar way to regular percent problems, except that instead of using the *part* you'll use the *amount of change*. Note that the sign of the *amount of change* is important: if the original amount has increased the change will be positive, and if it has decreased the change will be negative. Again, in the equations below the percent is a decimal value; you need to multiply by 100 to get the actual percentage.

$$percent\ change = \frac{amount\ of\ change}{original\ amount}$$

$$amount\ of\ change = original\ amount \times percent\ change$$

$$original\ amount = \frac{amount\ of\ change}{percent\ change}$$

Examples

1. A computer software retailer marks up its games by 40% above the wholesale price when it sells them to customers. Find the price of a game for a customer if the game costs the retailer $25.

Set up the appropriate equation and solve:

amount of change = *original amount* x *percent change* = 25 × 0.4 = 10

If the amount of change is 10, that means the store adds a markup of $10, so the game costs:

$25 + $10 = **$35**

2. A golf shop pays its wholesaler $40 for a certain club, and then sells it to a golfer for $75. What is the markup rate?

First, calculate the amount of change:

75 − 40 = 35

Now you can set up the equation and solve. (Note that *markup rate* is another way of saying *percent change*):

$$percent\ change = \frac{amount\ of\ change}{original\ amount} = \frac{35}{40} = 0.875 = \mathbf{87.5\%}$$

3. A store charges a 40% markup on the shoes it sells. How much did the store pay for a pair of shoes purchased by a customer for $63?

You're solving for the original price, but it's going to be tricky because you don't know the amount of change; you only know the new price. To solve, you need to create an expression for the amount of change:

If *original amount* = x

Then *amount of change* = 63 − x

Now you can plug these values into your equation:

$$original\ amount = \frac{amount\ of\ change}{percent\ change}$$

$$x = \frac{63-x}{0.4}$$

The last step is to solve for x:

$0.4x = 63 - x$

$1.4x = 63$

$x = 45$

The store paid **$45 for the shoes.**

4. An item originally priced at $55 is marked 25% off. What is the sale price?

You've been asked to find the sale price, which means you need to solve for the amount of change first:

amount   of   change   =   original   amount   ×   percent   change   →

55 × 0.25 = 13.75

69

Using this amount, you can find the new price. Because it's on sale, we know the item will cost less than the original price:
$$55 - 13.75 = 41.25$$
The sale price is $41.25.

5.   James wants to put in an 18 foot by 51 foot garden in his backyard. If he does, it will reduce the size of this yard by 24%. What will be the area of the remaining yard?
This problem is tricky because you need to figure out what each number in the problem stands for. 24% is obviously the percent change, but what about the measurements in feet? If you multiply these values you get the area of the garden (for more on area see *Area and Perimeter*):
$$18 \text{ ft.} \times 51 \text{ ft.} = 918 \text{ ft.}^2$$
This 918 ft.^{2} is the amount of change—it's how much smaller the lawn is. Now we can set up an equation:
$$original\ amount = \frac{amount\ of\ change}{percent\ change} = \frac{918}{0.24} = 3825$$
If the original lawn was 3825 ft.^{2} and the garden is 918 ft.^{2}, then the remaining area is
$$3825 - 918 = 2907$$
The remaining lawn covers **2907 ft.^{2}**

Probabilities

A **PROBABILITY** is found by dividing the number of desired outcomes by the number of total possible outcomes. As with percentages, a probability is the ratio of a part to a whole, with the whole being the total number of things that could happen, and the part being the number of those things that would be considered a success. Probabilities can be written using percentages (40%), decimals (0.4), fractions $\left(\frac{2}{5}\right)$, or in words (probability is 2 in 5).
$$probability = \frac{desired\ outcomes}{total\ possible\ outcomes}$$

Examples
1.   A bag holds 3 blue marbles, 5 green marbles, and 7 red marbles. If you pick one marble from the bag, what is the probability it will be blue?
Because there are 15 marbles in the bag (3 + 5 + 7), the total number of possible outcomes is 15. Of those outcomes, 3 would be blue marbles, which is the desired outcome. With that information you can set up an equation:
$$probability = \frac{desired\ outcomes}{total\ possible\ outcomes} = \frac{3}{15} = \frac{1}{5}$$
The probability is **1 in 5 or 0.2 that a blue marble is picked**.

2.   A bag contains 75 balls. If the probability that a ball selected from the bag will be red is 0.6, how many red balls are in the bag?
Because you're solving for desired outcomes (the number of red balls), first you need to rearrange the equation:
$$probability = \frac{desired\ outcomes}{total\ possible\ outcomes} \rightarrow$$
$$desired\ outcomes = probability \times total\ possible\ outcomes$$
In this problem, the desired outcome is choosing a red ball, and the total possible outcomes are represented by the 75 total balls.
$$desired\ outcomes = 0.6 \times 75 = 45$$
There are **45 red balls in the bag.**

3.   A theater has 230 seats: 75 seats are in the orchestra area, 100 seats are in the mezzanine, and 55 seats are in the balcony. If a ticket is selected at random, what is the probability that it will be for either a mezzanine or balcony seat?

In this problem, the desired outcome is a seat in either the mezzanine or balcony area, and the total possible outcomes are represented by the 230 total seats, so the equation should be written as:

$$probability = \frac{desired\ outcomes}{total\ possible\ outcomes} = \frac{100+55}{230} = \mathbf{0.67}$$

4.   The probability of selecting a student whose name begins with the letter *s* from a school attendance log is 7%. If there are 42 students whose names begin with *s* enrolled at the school, how many students attend the school?

Because you're solving for total possible outcomes (total number of students), first you need to rearrange the equation:

$$probability = \frac{desired\ outcomes}{total\ possible\ outcomes} \rightarrow$$

$$total\ possible\ outcomes = \frac{desired\ outcomes}{probability}$$

In this problem, you are given a probability (7% or 0.07) and the number of desired outcomes (42). These can be plugged into the equation to solve:

$$total\ possible\ outcomes = \frac{desired\ outcomes}{probability} = \frac{42}{0.07} = \mathbf{600\ students}$$

Algebra
Algebraic Expressions and Equations

Algebraic expressions and equations include a **VARIABLE**, which is a letter standing in for a number. These expressions and equations are made up of **TERMS**, which are groups of numbers and variables (e.g., $2xy$). An **EXPRESSION** is simply a set of terms (e.g., $3x + 2xy$), while an **EQUATION** includes an equal sign (e.g., $3x + 2xy = 17$). When simplifying expressions or solving algebraic equations, you'll need to use many different mathematical properties and operations, including addition, subtraction, multiplication, division, exponents, roots, distribution, and the order of operations.

Evaluating Algebraic Expressions

To evaluate an algebraic expression, simply plug the given value(s) in for the appropriate variable(s) in the expression.

Example

Evaluate $2x + 6y - 3z$ if , $x = 2$, $y = 4$, and $z = -3$.

Plug in each number for the correct variable and simplify:

$2x + 6y - 3z = 2(2) + 6(4) - 3(-3) = 4 + 24 + 9 = 37$

Adding and Subtracting Terms

Only like terms, which have the exact same variable(s), can be added or subtracted. Constants are numbers without variables attached, and those can be added and subtracted together as well. When simplifying an expression, like terms should be added or subtracted so that no individual group of variables occurs in more than one term. For example, the expression $5x + 6xy$ is in its simplest form, while $5x + 6xy - 11xy$ is not because the term xy appears more than once.

Example

71

Simplify the expression $5xy + 7y + 2yz + 11xy - 5yz$.
Start by grouping together like terms:
$(5xy + 11xy) + (2yz - 5yz) + 7y$
Now you can add together each set of like terms:
$16xy + 7y - 3yz$

Multiplying and Dividing Terms

To multiply a single term by another, simply multiply the coefficients and then multiply the variables. Remember that when multiplying variables with exponents, those exponents are added together. For example, $(x^5y)(x^3y^4) = x^8y^5$.

When multiplying a term by a set of terms inside parentheses, you need to **DISTRIBUTE** to each term inside the parentheses as shown below:

When variables occur in both the numerator and denominator of a fraction, they cancel each other out. So, a fraction with variables in its simplest form will not have the same variable on the top and bottom.

Examples

1.   Simplify the expression $(3x^4y^2z)(2y^4z^5)$.

Multiply the coefficients and variables together:

$3 \times 2 = 6$

$y^2 \times y^4 = y^6$

$z \times z^5 = z^6$

Now put all the terms back together:

$6x^4y^6z^6$

2.   Simplify the expression: $(2y^2)(y^3 + 2xy^2z + 4z)$

Multiply each term inside the parentheses by the term $2y^2$:

$(2y^2)(y^3 + 2xy^2z + 4z)$

$(2y^2 \times y^3) + (2y^2 \times 2xy^2z) \times (2y^2 \times 4z)$

$2y^5 + 4xy^4z + 8y^2z$

3.   Simplify the expression: $(5x + 2)(3x + 3)$

Use the acronym FOIL—First, Outer, Inner, Last—to multiply the terms:

First: $5x \times 3x = 15x^2$

Outer: $5x \times 3 = 15x$

Inner: $2 \times 3x = 6x$

Last: $2 \times 3 = 6$

Now combine like terms:

$15x^2 + 21x + 6$

4.   Simplify the expression: $\dfrac{2x^4y^3z}{8x^2z^3}$

Simplify by looking at each variable and crossing out those that appear in the numerator and denominator:

$\dfrac{2}{8} = \dfrac{1}{4}$

$\dfrac{x^4}{x^2} = \dfrac{x^2}{1}$

$\dfrac{z}{z^2} = \dfrac{1}{z}$

$\dfrac{2x^4y^3z}{8x^2z^3} = \dfrac{x^2y^3}{4z}$

Solving Equations

To solve an equation, you need to manipulate the terms on each side to isolate the variable, meaning if you want to find x, you have to get the x alone on one side of the equal sign. To do this, you'll need to use many of the tools discussed above: you might need to distribute, divide, add, or subtract like terms, or find common denominators.

Think of each side of the equation as the two sides of a see-saw. As long as the two people on each end weigh the same amount the see-saw will be balanced: if you have a 120 lb. person on each end, the see-saw is balanced. Giving each of them a 10 lb. rock to hold changes the weight on each end, but the see-saw itself stays balanced. Equations work the same way: you can add, subtract, multiply, or divide whatever you want as long as you do the same thing to both sides.

Most equations you'll see on the PARAPRO can be solved using the same basic steps:

1. Distribute to get rid of parentheses.
2. Use the least common denominator to get rid of fractions.
3. Add/subtract like terms on either side.
4. Add/subtract so that constants appear on only one side of the equation.
5. Multiply/divide to isolate the variable.

Examples

1. Solve for x: $25x + 12 = 62$

This equation has no parentheses, fractions, or like terms on the same side, so you can start by subtracting 12 from both sides of the equation:

$25x + 12 = 62$

$(25x + 12) - 12 = 62 - 12$

$25x = 50$

Now, divide by 25 to isolate the variable:

$\frac{25x}{25} = \frac{50}{25}$

$x = 2$

2. Solve the following equation for x: $2x - 4(2x + 3) = 24$

Start by distributing to get rid of the parentheses (don't forget to distribute the negative):

$2x - 4(2x + 3) = 24 \rightarrow$

$2x - 8x - 12 = 24$

There are no fractions, so now you can join like terms:

$2x - 8x - 12 = 24 \rightarrow$

$-6x - 12 = 24$

Now add 12 to both sides and divide by -6.

$-6x - 12 = 24$

$(-6x - 12) + 12 = 24 + 12 \rightarrow$

$-6x = 36 \rightarrow$

$\frac{-6x}{-6} = \frac{36}{-6}$

$x = -6$

3. Solve the following equation for x: $\frac{x}{3} + \frac{1}{2} = \frac{x}{6} - \frac{5}{12}$

Start by multiplying by the least common denominator to get rid of the fractions:

$\frac{x}{3} + \frac{1}{2} = \frac{x}{6} - \frac{5}{12} \rightarrow$

$12\left(\frac{x}{3} + \frac{1}{2}\right) = 12\left(\frac{x}{6} - \frac{5}{12}\right) \rightarrow$

$4x + 6 = 2x - 5$

Now you can isolate x:
$(4x + 6) - 6 = (2x - 5) - 6 \rightarrow$
$4x = 2x - 11 \rightarrow$
$(4x) - 2x = (2x - 11) - 2x \rightarrow$
$2x = -11 \rightarrow$
$x = \dfrac{11}{2}$

4. Find the value of x: $2(x + y) - 7x = 14x + 3$

This equation looks more difficult because it has 2 variables, but you can use the same steps to solve for x. First, distribute to get rid of the parentheses and combine like terms:
$2(x + y) - 7x = 14x + 3 \rightarrow$
$2x + 2y - 7x = 14x + 3 \rightarrow$
$-5x + 2y = 14x + 3$

Now you can move the x terms to one side and everything else to the other, and then divide to isolate x:
$-5x + 2y = 14x + 3 \rightarrow$
$-19x = -2y + 3 \rightarrow$
$x = \dfrac{2y - 3}{19}$

Inequalities

INEQUALITIES look like equations, except that instead of having an equal sign, they have one of the following symbols:

> Greater than: The expression left of the symbol is larger than the expression on the right.

< Less than: The expression left of the symbol is smaller than the expression on the right.

≥ Greater than or equal to: The expression left of the symbol is larger than or equal to the expression on the right.

≤ Less than or equal to: The expression left of the symbol is less than or equal to the expression on the right.

Inequalities are solved like linear and algebraic equations. The only difference is that the symbol must be reversed when both sides of the equation are multiplied by a negative number.

Example

Solve for x: $-7x + 2 < 6 - 5x$

Collect like terms on each side as you would for a regular equation:
$-7x + 2 < 6 - 5x \rightarrow$
$-2x < 4$

The direction of the sign switches when you divide by a negative number:
$-2x < 4 \rightarrow$
$x > -2$

Absolute Value

The ABSOLUTE VALUE of a number (represented by the symbol $|x|$) is its distance from zero, not its value. For example, $|3| = 3$, and $|-3| = 3$ because both 3 and -3 are three units from zero. The absolute value of a number is always positive.

Equations with absolute values will have two answers, so you need to set up two equations. The first is simply the equation with the absolute value symbol removed. For the second equation, isolate the absolute value on one side of the equation and multiply the other side of the equation by -1.

Examples

1.   Solve for x: $|2x - 3| = x + 1$

Set up the first equation by removing the absolute value symbol, then solve for x:

$|2x - 3| = x + 1$

$2x - 3 = x + 1$

$x = 4$

For the second equation, remove the absolute value and multiply by -1:

$|2x - 3| = x + 1 \rightarrow$

$2x - 3 = -(x + 1) \rightarrow$

$2x - 3 = -x - 1 \rightarrow$

$3x = 2$

$x = 2/3$

Both answers are correct, so the complete answer is $x = \mathbf{4}$ or $\frac{2}{3}$.

2.   Solve for y: $2|y + 4| = 10$

Set up the first equation:

$2(y + 4) = 10 \rightarrow$

$y + 4 = 5 \rightarrow$

$y = 1$

Set up the second equation. Remember to isolate the absolute value before multiplying by -1:

$2|y + 4| = 10 \rightarrow$

$|y + 4| = 5 \rightarrow$

$y + 4 = -5$

$y = -9$

$\mathbf{y = 1 \text{ or } -9}$

Solving Word Problems

Any of the math concepts discussed here can be turned into a word problem, and you'll likely see word problems in various forms throughout the test. (In fact, you may have noticed that several examples in the ratio and proportion sections were word problems.)

The most important step in solving any word problem is to read the entire problem before beginning to solve it: one of the most commonly made mistakes on word problems is providing an answer to a question that wasn't asked. Also, remember that not all of the information given in a problem is always needed to solve it.

When working multiple-choice word problems like those on the PARAPRO, it's important to check your answer. Many of the incorrect choices will be answers that test takers arrive at by making common mistakes. So even if an answer you calculated is given as an answer choice, that doesn't necessarily mean you've worked the problem correctly—you have to check your own work to make sure.

General Steps for Word Problem Solving

Step 1: Read the entire problem and determine what the question is asking for.

Step 2: List all of the given data and define the variables.

Step 3: Determine the formula(s) needed or set up equations from the information in the problem.

Step 4: Solve.

Step 5: Check your answer. (Is the amount too large or small? Are the answers in the correct unit of measure?)

Key Words

Word problems generally contain key words that can help you determine what math processes may be required in order to solve them.

- Addition: added, combined, increased by, in all, total, perimeter, sum, and more than
- Subtraction: how much more, less than, fewer than, exceeds, difference, and decreased
- Multiplication: of, times, area, and product
- Division: distribute, share, average, per, out of, percent, and quotient
- Equals: is, was, are, amounts to, and were

Basic Word Problems

A word problem in algebra is just an equation or a set of equations described using words. Your task when solving these problems is to turn the "story" of the problem into mathematical equations.

Examples

1.   A store owner bought a case of 48 backpacks for $476.00. He sold 17 of the backpacks in his store for $18 each, and the rest were sold to a school for $15 each. What was the salesman's profit?

Start by listing all the data and defining the variable:

total number of backpacks = 48

cost of backpacks = $476.00

backpacks sold in store at price of $18 = 17

backpacks sold to school at a price of $15 = 48 − 17 = 31

total profit = x

Now set up an equation:

total profit = income − cost = (306 + 465) − 476 = 295

The store owner made a profit of **$295**.

2.   Thirty students in Mr. Joyce's room are working on projects over 2 days. The first day, he gave them $\frac{3}{5}$ hour to work. On the second day, he gave them half as much time as the first day. How much time did each student have to work on the project?

Start by listing all the data and defining your variables. Note that the number of students, while given in the problem, is not needed to find the answer:

time on 1st day $= \frac{3}{5}$ hr. = 36 min.

time on 2nd day $= \frac{1}{2}(36) = 18$ min.

total time = x

Now set up the equation and solve:

total time = time on 1st day + time on 2nd day

$x = 36 + 18 = 54$

The students had **54 minutes** to work on the projects.

Distance Word Problems

Distance word problems involve something traveling at a constant or average speed. Whenever you read a problem that involves *how fast*, *how far*, or *for how long*, you should think of the distance equation, $d = rt$, where d stands for distance, r for rate (speed), and t for time.

These problems can be solved by setting up a grid with d, r, and t along the top and each moving object on the left. When setting up the grid, make sure the units are consistent. For example, if the distance is in meters and the time is in seconds, the rate should be meters per second.

Examples

1. Will drove from his home to the airport at an average speed of 30 mph. He then boarded a helicopter and flew to the hospital with an average speed of 60 mph. The entire distance was 150 miles, and the trip took 3 hours. Find the distance from the airport to the hospital.

The first step is to set up a table and fill in a value for each variable:

DRIVE TIME			
	d	r	t
driving	d	30	t
flying	$150 - d$	60	$3 - t$

You can now set up equations for driving and flying. The first row gives the equation $d = 30t$, and the second row gives the equation $150 - d = 60(3 - t)$.

Next, you can solve this system of equations. Start by substituting for d in the second equation:

$d = 30t$

$150 - d = 60(3 - t) \rightarrow 150 - 30t = 60(3 - t)$

Now solve for t:

$150 - 30t = 180 - 60t$

$-30 = -30t$

$1 = t$

Although you've solved for t, you're not done yet. Notice that the problem asks for distance. So, you need to solve for d: what the problem asked for. It does not ask for time, but the time is needed to solve the problem.

Driving: $30t = 30$ miles

Flying: $150 - d = 120$ miles

The distance from the airport to the hospital is **120 miles**.

2. Two cyclists start at the same time from opposite ends of a course that is 45 miles long. One cyclist is riding at 14 mph and the second cyclist is riding at 16 mph. How long after they begin will they meet?

First, set up the table. The variable for time will be the same for each, because they will have been on the road for the same amount of time when they meet:

CYCLIST TIMES			
	d	r	t
Cyclist #1	d	14	t
Cyclist #2	$45 - d$	16	t

Next set up two equations:

Cyclist #1: $d = 14t$
Cyclist #2: $45 - d = 16t$
Now substitute and solve:
$d = 14t$
$45 - d = 16t \rightarrow 45 - 14t = 16t$
$45 = 30t$
$t = 1.5$
They will meet **1.5 hr.** after they begin.

Work Problems

WORK PROBLEMS involve situations where several people or machines are doing work at different rates. Your task is usually to figure out how long it will take these people or machines to complete a task while working together. The trick to doing work problems is to figure out how much of the project each person or machine completes in the same unit of time. For example, you might calculate how much of a wall a person can paint in 1 hour, or how many boxes an assembly line can pack in 1 minute.

Once you know that, you can set up an equation to solve for the total time. This equation usually has a form similar to the equation for distance, but here *work – rate × time*.

Examples

1.   Bridget can clean an entire house in 12 hours while her brother Tom takes 8 hours. How long would it take for Bridget and Tom to clean 2 houses together?

Start by figuring out how much of a house each sibling can clean on his or her own. Bridget can clean the house in 12 hours, so she can clean $\frac{1}{12}$ of the house in an hour. Using the same logic, Tom can clean $\frac{1}{8}$ of a house in an hour.

By adding these values together, you get the fraction of the house they can clean together in an hour:
$\frac{1}{12} + \frac{1}{8} = \frac{5}{24}$

They can do $\frac{5}{24}$ of the job per hour.

Now set up variables and an equation to solve:
t = time spent cleaning (in hours)
h = number of houses cleaned = 2
work = rate × time
$h = \frac{5}{24}t \rightarrow$
$2 = \frac{5}{24}t \rightarrow$
$t = \frac{48}{5} = 9\frac{3}{5}$ **hours**

2.   Farmer Dan needs to water his cornfield. One hose can water a field 1.25 times faster than a second hose. When both hoses are opened, they water the field in 5 hours. How long would it take to water the field if only the second hose is used?

In this problem you don't know the exact time, but you can still find the hourly rate as a variable:

The first hose completes the job in f hours, so it waters $\frac{1}{f}$ field per hour. The slower hose waters the field in $1.25f$, so it waters the field in $\frac{1}{1.25f}$ hours. Together, they take 5 hours to water the field, so they water $\frac{1}{5}$ of the field per hour.

Now you can set up the equations and solve:
$\frac{1}{f} + \frac{1}{1.25f} = \frac{1}{5} \rightarrow$

$$1.25f\left(\frac{1}{f}+\frac{1}{1.25f}\right)=1.25f\left(\frac{1}{5}\right)\rightarrow$$
$$1.25+1=0.25f$$
$$2.25=0.25f$$
$$f=9$$

The fast hose takes 9 hours to water the cornfield. The slower hose takes $1.25(9) =$ **11.25 hours**.

3. Alex takes 2 hours to shine 500 silver spoons, and Julian takes 3 hours to shine 450 silver spoons. How long will they take, working together, to shine 1000 silver spoons?

Calculate how many spoons each man can shine per hour:

Alex: $\dfrac{500\text{ spoons}}{2\text{ hours}}=\dfrac{250\text{ spoons}}{1\text{ hour}}$

Julian: $\dfrac{450\text{ spoons}}{3\text{ hours}}=\dfrac{150\text{ spoons}}{1\text{ hour}}$

Together: $\dfrac{(250+150)}{1\text{ hour}}=\dfrac{400\text{ spoons}}{1\text{ hour}}$

Now set up an equation to find the time it takes to shine 1000 spoons:

$$\text{total time}=\dfrac{1\text{ hour}}{400\text{ spoons}}\times 1000\text{ spoons}=\dfrac{1000}{40}\text{ hours}=\mathbf{2.5\text{ hours}}$$

Statistics and Geometry
Graphs and Charts

These questions require you to interpret information from graphs and charts; they will be pretty straightforward as long as you pay careful attention to detail. There are several different graph and chart types that may appear on the PARAPRO.

Bar Graphs

BAR GRAPHS present the numbers of an item that exist in different categories. The categories are shown on the *x*-axis, and the number of items is shown on the *y*-axis. Bar graphs are usually used to easily compare amounts.

Examples

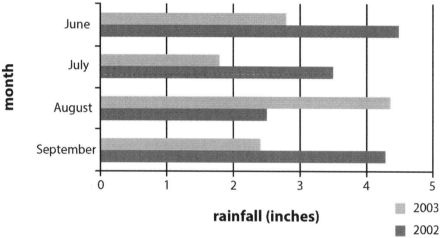

1.   The graph above shows rainfall in inches per month. Which month had the least amount of rainfall? Which had the most?

The shortest bar represents the month with the least rain, and the longest bar represents the month with the most rain: **July 2003 had the least**, and **June 2002 had the most**.

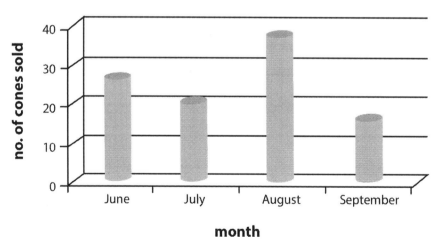

2.   Using the graph above, how many more ice cream cones were sold in July than in September? Tracing from the top of each bar to the scale on the left shows that sales in July were 20 and September sales were 15. So, **5 more cones were sold in July**.

81

Pie Charts

PIE CHARTS present parts of a whole, and are often used with percentages. Together, all the slices of the pie add up to the total number of items, or 100%.

Examples

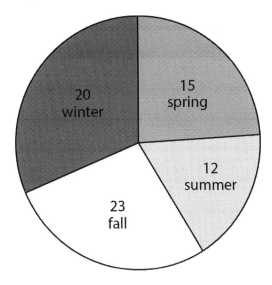

1. The pie chart above shows the distribution of birthdays in a class of students. How many students have birthdays in the spring or summer?

Fifteen students have birthdays in spring and 12 in winter, so there are **27 students** with birthdays in spring or summer.

2. Using the same Birthday Pie Chart in the example before, what percentage of students have birthdays in winter?

Use the equation for percent:

$$percent = \frac{part}{whole} = \frac{winter\ birthdays}{total\ birthdays} = \frac{20}{20+15+23+12} = \frac{20}{70} = \frac{2}{7} = \mathbf{0.286}\ or\ \mathbf{28.6\%}$$

Line Graphs

LINE GRAPHS show trends over time. The number of each item represented by the graph will be on the *y*-axis, and time will be on the *x*-axis.

Examples

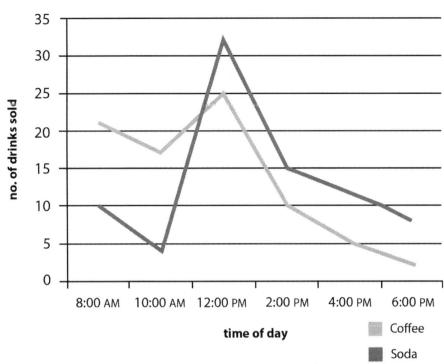

1. The line graph above shows beverage sales at an airport snack shop throughout the day. Which beverage sold more at 4:00 p.m.?

At 4:00 p.m., approximately 12 sodas and 5 coffees were sold, so more **soda** was sold.

2. At what time of day were the most beverages sold?

This question is asking for the time of day with the most sales of coffee and soda combined. It is not necessary to add up sales at each time of day to find the answer. Just from looking at the graph, you can see that sales for both beverages were highest at noon, so the answer must be **12:00 p.m.**

Mean, Median, and Mode

MEAN is a math term for average. To find the mean, total all the terms and divide by the number of terms. The **MEDIAN** is the middle number of a given set. To find the median, put the terms in numerical order; the middle number will be the median. In the case of a set of even numbers, the middle two numbers are averaged. **MODE** is the number which occurs most frequently within a given set.

Examples

1. Find the mean of 24, 27, and 18.

Add the terms, then divide by the number of terms:

$$mean = \frac{24+27+18}{3} = 23$$

2. The mean of three numbers is 45. If two of the numbers are 38 and 43, what is the third number?

Set up the equation for mean with x representing the third number, then solve:

$$mean = \frac{38+43+x}{3} = 45$$
$$38 + 43 + x = 135$$
$$x = 54$$

3. What is the median of 24, 27, and 18?

Place the terms in order, then pick the middle term:

18, 24, 27

The median is **24**.

4. What is the median of 24, 27, 18, and 19?

Place the terms in order. Because there are an even number of terms, the median will be the average of the middle 2 terms:

18, 19, 24, 27

$$median = \frac{19+24}{2} = \mathbf{21.5}$$

5. What is the mode of 2, 5, 4, 4, 3, 2, 8, 9, 2, 7, 2, and 2?
The mode is **2** because it appears the most within the set.

Area and Perimeter

AREA and PERIMETER problems will require you to use the equations shown in the table below to find either the area inside a shape or the distance around it (the perimeter). These equations will not be given on the test, so you need to have them memorized on test day.

EQUATIONS		
shape	**area**	**perimeter**
circle	$A = \pi r^2$	$C = 2\pi r = \pi d$
triangle	$A = \dfrac{b \times h}{2}$	$P = s_1 + s_2 + s_3$
square	$A = s^2$	$P = 4s$
rectangle	$A = l \times w$	$P = 2l + 2w$

Examples

1. A farmer has purchased 100 m of fencing to put around his rectangular garden. If one side of the garden is 20 m long and the other is 28 m, how much fencing will the farmer have left over?
The perimeter of a rectangle is equal to twice its length plus twice its width:
P = 2(20) + 2(28) = 96 m
The farmer has 100 m of fencing, so he'll have 100 – 96 = **4 m left**

2. Taylor is going to paint a square wall that is 3.5 m tall. What is the total area that Taylor will be painting?
Each side of the square wall is 3.5 m:
$A = 3.5^2 =$ **12.25 m²**

Pythagorean Theorem

Shapes with 3 sides are known as TRIANGLES. In addition to knowing the formulas for their area and perimeter, you should also know the Pythagorean theorem, which describes the relationship between the three sides (a, b, and c) of a right triangle:

$a^2 + b^2 = c^2$

Example

Erica is going to run a race in which she'll run 3 miles due north and 4 miles due east. She'll then run back to the starting line. How far will she run during this race?

One leg of her route (the triangle) is missing, but you can find its length using the Pythagorean theorem:

$a^2 + b^2 = c^2$

$3^2 + 4^2 = c^2$

$25 = c^2$

$c = 5$

Adding all 3 sides gives the length of the whole race:

$3 + 4 + 5 = 12$ miles

Test Your Knowledge: The Math Section

1. Melissa has been thinking about buying a car. She estimates that she would spend $200 per month on car payments, $25 per week on gas, and $600 per year on insurance. About how much would she spend per month? (Note: a month contains four weeks.)
    - A) $125
    - B) $275
    - C) $350
    - D) $825

2. Mary works from 5:00 p.m. to 8:30 p.m. on Wednesdays and Thursdays, and from 9:00 a.m. to 3:30 p.m. on Saturdays and Sundays. How many hours does Mary work per week?
    - A) 10
    - B) 20
    - C) 18
    - D) 14.5

3. A car rental company charges a daily fee of $48 plus 25% of the daily fee for every hour the car is late. If you rent a car for 2 days and bring it back 2 hours late, what will be the total charge?
    - A) $120
    - B) $108
    - C) $72
    - D) $144

4. Rebecca, Emily, and Kate all live on the same straight road. Rebecca lives 1.4 miles from Kate and 0.8 miles from Emily. What is the minimum distance Emily could live from Kate?
    - A) 2.2 miles
    - B) 1.1 miles
    - C) 0.8 miles
    - D) 0.6 miles

5. Alex, David, and Rachel go out to dinner. Alex and David decide to split an appetizer that costs $8.50, and Rachel gets her own appetizer that costs $6.50. Rachel orders lemonade that costs $3, while Alex and David drink the free water. They all order entrées that cost the same price. They split up the bill according to what each person ordered; how much less (before tax and tip) will Alex and David each pay compared to Rachel?
    - A) $5.25
    - B) $1.00
    - C) $5.00
    - D) $7.25

6. During a recent storm, it snowed at a rate of 2 centimeters per hour for 190 minutes, 4 centimeters per hour for 40 minutes, 1 centimeter per hour for 280 minutes, and 3 millimeters per hour for 50 minutes. What was the total snowfall to the nearest centimeter?
    - A) 13 centimeters
    - B) 10 centimeters
    - C) 16 centimeters
    - D) 14 centimeters

7. A car dealership is offering huge deals for the weekend. The commercials claim that this year's models are 20% off the list price, and the dealership will pay the first 3 monthly payments. If a car is listed for $26,580, and the monthly payments are set at $250, what are the total potential savings?
    A) $20,514
    B) $5,566
    C) $6,066
    D) $1,282

8. To get to work, Matt walks 0.75 miles from his house to the bus stop and rides the bus 3.8 miles to his office. If he walks at a pace of 3.6 miles per hour and the bus drives at an average speed of 15 miles per hour, what is his total commute time? (Assume he spends no time waiting for the bus.)
    A) 27 minutes, 42 seconds
    B) 27 minutes, 7 seconds
    C) 46 minutes, 16 seconds
    D) 1 hour, 6 minutes, 20 seconds

9. There are 450 students in the 10th grade; of these, 46% are boys. If 21% of the girls have already turned 16, how many girls in the 10th grade are 16?
    A) 47
    B) 94
    C) 51
    D) 10

10. Joe baked brownies in a 9 inch × 11 inch × 2 inch tray. He then cut the brownies into 12 large pieces. Joe ate 2 pieces, his roommate ate 3 pieces, and the dog unfortunately ate half of what was remaining. Joe now has to bring the dog to the vet. When the vet asks what volume of brownies dog ate, what should Joe tell him?
    A) 99 in^3
    B) 57.75 in^3
    C) 82.5 in^3
    D) 115.5 in^3

11. There are 32 cabins at a summer camp: 16 for boys and 16 for girls. Each cabin has 4 bunk beds, sleeping 8 people in total. There are 76 boys registered for camp; the number of girls registered is 25% greater than the number of boys. If campers are assigned to cabins while using the fewest number of cabins possible (still keeping boys and girls separate), how many boys and girls will stay in unfilled cabins?
    A) 9 boys and 11 girls
    B) 9 boys and 3 girls
    C) 4 boys and 7 girls
    D) 4 boys and 3 girls

12. You are buying supplies for your class cookout. You are expecting 32 students and 2 teachers to attend. You estimate that for every 3 people, you will need 5 hamburgers. The hamburger patties come in packs of 6. How many packs should you buy?
    A) 10 packs
    B) 9 packs
    C) 8 packs

88

D)   4 packs

13. One-way city bus tickets cost $1.75. The transportation department offers a monthly bus pass for $48. During the week, Jun commutes to work roundtrip on the bus. If Jun bought the monthly pass, how many days would he have to commute per month in order to save money?
    A)   28
    B)   14
    C)   13
    D)   7

14. The county is instituting a new license plate system. The new plates will have 6 digits: the first digit will be 1, 2 or 3, and the next 5 digits can be any number from 0 – 9. How many possible unique combinations does this new system offer?
    A) 3×10^5
    B) 3×10^6
    C) 10^6
    D)   53

15. Jill worked 8 hours on Monday, 9.5 hours on Tuesday, 8 hours on Wednesday, 10 hours on Thursday, and 9 hours on Friday. She is paid $16.50 per hour, and she receives 1.5 times her normal rate for overtime hours (any hours over 40 hours per week). How much will she be paid this week?
    A) $734.25
    B) $1,064.25
    C) $1,101.38
    D) $771.38

16. Grace has been watching airline ticket prices before booking her trip. When she checked prices yesterday, they were down 15% from the day before. When she looked again today, they had risen 5% since yesterday. What is the percentage difference since the first time she looked at prices?
    A)   −19.25%
    B)   −10.00%
    C)   −10.75%
    D)   +9.25%

17. The high temperature on Wednesday is 4 degrees warmer than the high temperature on Tuesday, which was 5 degrees cooler than the high temperature on Monday. If the high temperature on Thursday is predicted to be 3 degrees cooler than the high on Wednesday, what is the difference in temperature between Monday and Thursday?
    A)   3 degrees
    B)   4 degrees
    C)   6 degrees
    D)   12 degrees

18. George is reselling his used textbooks. He originally bought the books new for $164. He sells them used for $108, plus $16 in shipping and handling. He pays $11.25 for shipping. How much does George profit?
    A)   George makes a profit of $60.75.
    B)   George makes a profit of $51.25.
    C)   George does not make a profit; he has lost $51.25.

D)   George does not make a profit; he has lost $60.75.

19. When Drew rides the bus to school, it takes 16 minutes. When Drew makes the same trip on his bicycle, it takes 24 minutes. How much faster is the bus than his bike?
    A)   1.5 times faster
    B)   2.5 times faster
    C)   2 times faster
    D)   3 times faster

20. A dry cleaner charges $3 per shirt, $6 per pair of pants, and an extra $5 per item for mending. Annie drops off 5 shirts and 4 pairs of pants, 2 of which needed mending. Assuming the cleaner charges an 8% sales tax, what will be Annie's total bill?
    A) $52.92
    B) $49.00
    C) $45.08
    D) $88.20

21. Mary and Phil are practicing their basketball free-throws. Each takes 20 shots. Mary makes 15 of her shots, while Phil makes 12. Based on this performance, what is Mary's probability of making a free-throw?
    A)   1.25
    B)   0.6
    C)   0.75
    D)   0.25

22. A faucet is leaking 1 drop every 4 seconds. If 1 gallon is equal to 15,140 drops, how long will it take for this faucet to leak 1 gallon of water?
    A)   4 hours, 12 minutes, 20 seconds
    B)   1 hour, 3 minutes, 5 seconds
    C)   16 hours, 49 minutes, 20 seconds
    D)   18 hours, 24 minutes, 5 seconds

23. A recipe for cookies uses 4.5 cups of flour and claims to serve 12 people. The recipe assumes that one serving size is 2 cookies. If you have 5 friends and you want to make enough for everyone (including yourself) to have 3 cookies, how much flour should you use?
    A) $1\frac{1}{2}$ cups
    B) $2\frac{1}{2}$ cups
    C)   6 cups
    D) $3\frac{3}{8}$ cups

24. Your car's gas tank is a quarter full. Assuming the tank holds 10 gallons, and your car gets an average of 26 miles per gallon, how many miles can you drive before you run out of gas?
    A)   260 miles
    B)   65 miles
    C)   6.5 miles
    D)   10.4 miles

25. Caroline's basketball coach has the team run ladder sprints at practice. They run from the near end line to the free-throw line, back to the near end line, up to the center division line, back to the near end line, out to the far end line, and finish back at the near end line. If the distances from the end line to the free-throw line is 19 feet and the distance from the free-throw line to the center division line is 28 feet, how long is one ladder sprint?
    A)   160 feet
    B)   206 feet
    C)   320 feet
    D)   396 feet

26. Power is a measure of energy expenditure over time. Watts, a measure of power, are equal to energy in joules over time in seconds. If a 40-watt light bulb is left on for 4.5 hours, how much energy is consumed?
    A)   648 kilojoules
    B)   6480 joules
    C)   108 kilojoules
    D)   180 joules

27. Mike is training for a marathon (26.2 miles) and wants to cut his current time from 3 hours, 50 minutes to 3 hours, 42 minutes. By how much should he cut his time per mile?
    A)   48.3 seconds/mile
    B)   8 minutes/mile
    C)   30.5 seconds/mile
    D)   18.3 seconds/mile

28. A summer camp requires a ratio of 1 camp counselor to every 6 campers. Each camp counselor makes $480 per week. If the camp director wants to register an additional 30 campers for 2 weeks this summer, how much more will she have to budget to pay counselors?
    A) $2,400
    B) $4,800
    C) $5,760
    D) $2,880

29. The owner of a newspaper has noticed that print subscriptions have gone down 40% while online subscriptions have gone up 60%. If print subscriptions once accounted for 70% of the newspaper's business, and online subscriptions accounted for 25%, what is the overall percentage growth or decline in business?
    A)   28% growth
    B)   13% decline
    C)   15% decline
    D)   Business has stayed the same.

30. Leah is 4 inches taller than Zach, who is 10% taller than Ben. If Ben is 48 inches tall, how much taller is Leah than Ben?
    A)   8.8 inches
    B)   0.8 inches
    C)   9.2 inches
    D)   6.1 inches

31. Adam is shopping the clearance section at his favorite department store. He finds a jacket that is marked $\frac{1}{3}$ off. His student discount gives him an additional $\frac{1}{5}$ off the original price. By what fraction is the jacket discounted in total?

    A) $\frac{1}{15}$

    B) $\frac{6}{15}$

    C) $\frac{7}{15}$

    D) $\frac{8}{15}$

32. On Monday, Grace fills the gas tank of her car up to $\frac{3}{4}$ full. On Tuesday, she uses $\frac{1}{8}$ of a tank, on Wednesday she uses $\frac{3}{16}$ of a tank, and on Thursday she uses another $\frac{1}{4}$ of a tank. What fraction of the gas tank is full after Thursday?

    A) $\frac{3}{16}$

    B) $\frac{7}{16}$

    C) $\frac{13}{16}$

    D) $\frac{1}{4}$

33. Based on a favorable performance review at work, Matt receives a $\frac{3}{20}$ increase in his hourly wage. If his original hourly wage is represented by w, express his new wage in decimal form.

    A) $0.15w$

    B) $0.85w$

    C) $1.12w$

    D) $1.15w$

34. Express $\frac{15}{25}$ as a decimal.

    A)   0.15

    B)   0.06

    C)   0.6

    D)   0.375

35. How many cents is $\frac{8}{11}$ of a dollar?

    A)   0.73

    B)   0.72

    C)   0.81

    D)   0.79

36. Stephanie eats 0.625 of her pizza. If her pizza was cut into 8 slices, how many slices has she eaten?

    A)   3

    B)   4

    C)   5

    D)   6

37. A carnival game involves picking rubber ducks with numbers written on the bottom. There is a 0.05 probability of picking a rubber duck with the number 3. What fraction of the rubber ducks are numbered 3?

    A) $\frac{1}{20}$

    B) $\frac{3}{20}$

    C) $\frac{1}{5}$

    D) $\frac{1}{15}$

38. A chocolate chip cookie recipe calls for 2.375 cups of flour. Express this quantity as a fraction.

    A) $2\frac{3}{5}$ cups

    B) $2\frac{3}{8}$ cups

    C) $2\frac{2}{8}$ cups

    D) $2\frac{1}{3}$ cups

39. A marinade recipe calls for 2 tablespoons of lemon juice for $\frac{1}{4}$ cup of olive oil. How much lemon juice should you use with $\frac{2}{3}$ cup olive oil?

    A) $5\frac{1}{3}$ tablespoons

    B) $\frac{3}{4}$ tablespoons

    C)   4 tablespoons

    D) $2\frac{1}{3}$ tablespoons

40. A material's specific heat capacity is the amount of energy needed to increase the temperature of 1 gram of that material by 1 degree Celsius. If the specific heat capacity of aluminum is $0.900\frac{J}{g \cdot °C}$, how many joules of energy does it take to increase the temperature of 2 grams of aluminum by 4 degrees Celsius?

    A)   3.6 joules

    B)   0.1 joules

    C)   7.2 joules

    D)   5.6 joules

41. The density of cork is approximately 0.24 grams per cubic centimeter. How much water would 100 grams of cork displace?

    A)   3.67 cm^3

    B)   1.24 cm^3

    C)   24 cm^3

    D)   4.17 cm^3

42. Stephanie's car uses an average of 29 miles per gallon. $\frac{1}{3}$ of her gas tank holds 3.5 gallons. How many miles can she drive on a full tank of gas?

    A)   33.8 miles

    B)   101.5 miles

    C)   367.5 miles

D)   304.5 miles

43. Adam owns 4 times as many shirts as he has pairs of pants, and he has 5 pairs of pants for every 2 pairs of shoes. What is the ratio of Adam's shirts to Adam's shoes?
   A)   25 shirts : 1 pair shoes
   B)   10 shirts : 1 pair shoes
   C)   20 shirts : 1 pair shoes
   D)   15 shirts : 2 pairs shoes

44. A box of instant rice provides the following instructions: "For 4 servings, stir 2 cups of rice into 1.75 cups of boiling water." How many cups of water are needed for 6 servings of rice?
   A)   2.625 cups
   B)   13.7 cups
   C)   3 cups
   D)   1.167 cups

45. A restaurant employs servers, hosts, and managers in a ratio of 9:2:1. If there are 36 total employees, how many hosts are there?
   A)   4
   B)   3
   C)   6
   D)   8

46. After a big snow storm, Maria and her brother Bill work together for 3 hours to shovel snow off their driveway and sidewalk. If the total area is 90 square feet, and the snow accumulation is 18 inches, what is the ratio of snow volume shoveled to 1 man hour?
   A) 22.5 ft^3 : 1 man hour
   B) 15 ft^3 : 1 man hour
   C) 270 ft^3 : 1 man hour
   D) 45 ft^3 : 1 man hour

47. 7 is what percent of 60?
   A)   11.67%
   B)   4.20%
   C)   8.57%
   D)   10.11%

48. What percent of 14 is 35?
   A)   4.9%
   B)   2.5%
   C)   40%
   D)   250%

49. 15 is 8 percent of what number?
   A)   1.2
   B)   53.3
   C)   187.5
   D)   120

50. On a given day at the local airport, 15 flights were delayed and 62 left on time. What percentage of the flights was delayed?
    A)   24.2%
    B)   19.5%
    C)   80.5%
    D)   22.4%

51. Gym A offers a monthly membership for 80% of the cost at Gym B; the cost at Gym B is 115% the cost at Gym C. What percentage of the cost at Gym C does Gym A charge?
    A)   35%
    B)   97%
    C)   70%
    D)   92%

52. If there are 380 female students in a graduating class, and male students represent 60% of the graduating class, how many total students are there in the class?
    A)   633
    B)   950
    C)   570
    D)   720

53. What is 18% of 76% of 15,000?
    A)   3,553
    B)   2,052
    C)   633
    D)   8,700

54. A manufacturer sells a product to a retailer for 350% of the production cost. The retailer sells the product to consumers for 600% of the production cost. What percentage of her purchase cost is the retailer's profit when she sells to consumers?
    A)   250%
    B)   41.7%
    C)   58.3%
    D)   71.4%

55. Evaluate the expression $\frac{4x}{x-1}$ when $x = 5$.
    A)   3
    B)   4
    C)   5
    D)   6

56. Evaluate the expression $\frac{x^2-2y}{y}$ when $x = 20$ and $y = \frac{x}{2}$.
    A)   0
    B)   38
    C)   36
    D)   19

57. Evaluate the expression $\sqrt{(x^{-1})4x}$ when $x = y + 3$ and $y = 14$.

    A)   2

    B) -2

    C)   34

    D) $\dfrac{1}{\sqrt{2}}$

58. Simplify: $3x^3 + 4x - (2x + 5y) + y$

    A) $3x^3 + 2x + y$

    B) $11x - 4y$

    C) $3x^3 + 2x - 4y$

    D) $29x - 4y$

59. Find the sum: $2\left(\dfrac{y}{x}\right) + \dfrac{1}{x}(3y)$

    A) $\dfrac{y}{x}$

    B) $\dfrac{5y}{x^2}$

    C) $\dfrac{5y}{6x}$

    D) $\dfrac{5y}{x}$

60. Simplify the expression: $x^3 - 3x^2 + (2x)^3 - x$

    A) $x^3 - 3x^2 + 7x$

    B) $9x^3 - 3x^2 - x$

    C) $20x$

    D) $7x^3 - 3x^2 - x$

61. What is the range of the function $f(x) = x^2 + 2$?

    A)   all real numbers

    B)   all real numbers greater than 2

    C)   all real numbers greater than or equal to 2

    D)   all real numbers less than or equal to 2

62. Consider the function $f(x) = -2x - 5$ with the range $\{17, 15, 11, -5\}$. Define the domain.

    A)   domain $= \{-11, -10, -8, 0\}$

    B)   domain $= \{-39, -35, -27, 5\}$

    C)   domain $= \{-14, -11, -6, 0\}$

    D)   domain $= \{-6, -5, -3, 5\}$

63. Which of the following is always true of functions?

    A)   For each value in the range, there is only one value in the domain.

    B)   For each value in the domain, there is only one value in the range.

    C)   The range of a function includes all real numbers.

    D)   The domain of a function includes all real numbers.

64. If $f(x) = 3^x - 2$, evaluate $f(5)$.

A) 27
B) 243
C) 241
D) 13

65. Which of the following is true of the function $f(x) = 8^x$?
   A)   The graph of the function has a horizontal asymptote along the negative x-axis.
   B)   The graph of the function has a horizontal asymptote along the positive x-axis.
   C)   The graph of the function has a vertical asymptote along the negative y-axis.
   D)   The graph of the function has a vertical asymptote along the positive y-axis.

66. If $f(x) = 0.5^x + 1$, evaluate $f(-2)$.

   A) 0.75
   B) 2
   C) 4
   D) 5

67. If $f(x) = e^{2x}$, evaluate $\ln[f(3)]$.

   A) 3
   B) 5
   C) 6
   D) $\dfrac{1}{e^6}$

68. Which of the following is true of the function $f(x) = 1^x - 3$?

   A) The graph of the function is a horizontal line at $y = -2$.
   B) The graph of the function is a vertical line at $x = -2$.
   C) The graph of the function has a horizontal asymptote at $y = -3$.
   D) The graph of the function has a vertical asymptote at $x = -3$.

69. A 650 square foot apartment in Boston costs $1800 per month to rent. What is the monthly rent per square foot?

   A) $13
   B) $0.36
   C) $2.77
   D) $3.66

70. A radio station plays songs that last an average of 3.5 minutes and has commercial breaks that last 2 minutes. If the station is required to play 1 commercial break for every 4 songs, how many songs can the station play in an hour?

   A) 15
   B) 11
   C) 16
   D) 17

71. Students in a particular math class received an average score of 84% on a recent test. If there are 20 boys and 30 girls in the class, and the boys' average score was 82%, what was the girls' average score?

   A) 83%
   B) 88%
   C) 85%
   D) 86%

72. $\frac{1}{10}$ of a company's employees are in their 20s, $\frac{2}{5}$ are in their 30s, $\frac{1}{3}$ are in their 40s and the remaining 5 employees are 50 or older. How many employees work at the company?

    A)   5
    B)   30
    C)   60
    D)   24

73. A chemical experiment requires that a solute be diluted with 4 parts (by mass) water for every 1 part (by mass) solute. If the desired mass for the solution is 90 grams, how much solute should be used?

    A)   15 grams
    B)   72 grams
    C)   22.5 grams
    D)   18 grams

74. Lisa rides her bike at 10 miles per hour for 28 minutes, 15 miles per hour for 49 minutes, and 12 miles per hour for 15 minutes. How far did she travel in total?

    A)   11.95 miles
    B)   18.91 miles
    C)   19.92 miles
    D)   20.21 miles

75. A plane makes a trip of 246 miles. For some amount of time, the plane's speed is 115 miles per hour. For the remainder of the trip, the plane's speed is 250 miles per hour. If the total trip time is 72 minutes, how long did the plane fly at 115 miles per hour?

    A)   18 minutes
    B)   23 minutes
    C)   24 minutes
    D)   34 minutes

76. A runner completes a 12 mile race in 1 hour and 30 minutes. If her pace for the first part of the race was 7 minutes per mile, and her pace for the second part of the race was 8 minutes per mile, for how many miles did she sustain her pace of 7 minutes per mile?

    A)   4 miles
    B)   5.5 miles
    C)   6 miles
    D)   7 miles

77. A swimmer is swimming 25 meter sprints. If he swims 4 sprints in 3 minutes, 6 more sprints in 5 minutes, and then 4 final sprints in 2 minutes, what was his average speed during his sprints?

    A)   35 meters per minute
    B)   1.4 meters per minute
    C)   350 meters per minute
    D)   17.9 meters per minute

78. A cheetah in the wild can accelerate from 0 miles per hour to 60 miles per hour in 2.8 seconds. Then, it can sustain a speed of 60 miles per hour for up to 60 seconds before it has to rest. How much total distance can the cheetah travel from when it starts to accelerate to the moment it has to stop?

    A)   3,684 miles
    B)   2.4 miles
    C)   1.046 miles
    D)   1.023 miles

79. 2 warehouse workers can pack 5 boxes in 6 minutes. If 1 worker can pack 6 boxes by himself in 15 minutes, how many boxes can the other worker pack by himself in the same amount of time?

    A)   6.5 boxes
    B)   6 boxes
    C)   12.5 boxes
    D)   7.5 boxes

80. John and Jake are working at a car wash. It takes John 1 hour to wash 3 cars; Jake can wash 3 cars in 45 minutes. If they work together, how many cars can they wash in 1 hour?

    A)   6 cars
    B)   7 cars
    C)   9 cars
    D)   12 cars

81. Ed is going to fill his swimming pool with a garden hose. His neighbor, a volunteer firefighter, wants to use a fire hose attached to the hydrant in the front yard to make the job go faster. The fire hose sprays 13.5 times as much water per minute as the garden hose. If the garden hose and the fire hose together can fill the pool in 107 minutes, how long would it have taken to fill the pool with the garden hose alone?

    A)   7 hours, 37.9 min
    B)   7 hours, 55.6 min
    C)   1 day, 4.5 min
    D)   1 day, 1 hour, 51.5 min

82. Suppose Mark can mow the entire lawn in 47 minutes, and Mark's dad can mow the entire lawn in 53 minutes. If Mark and his dad work together (each with their own lawnmowers), how long will it take them to mow the entire lawn?

    A)   15.6 minutes
    B)   24.9 minutes
    C)   26.5 minutes
    D)   50 minutes

83. Rafael and Marco are repainting their garage. If Rafael can paint 1/6 of the garage in 20 minutes, and Marco can paint 1/5 of the garage in 30 minutes, how long will it take them to paint the entire garage if they work together?

    A)   1 hr, 6.7 min
    B)   2 hr, 43.6 min
    C)   0 hr, 54 min
    D)   6 hr, 12 min

84. Find the area of a rectangular athletic field that is 100 meters long and 45 meters wide.

    A)   290 meters
    B)   4,500 m^2
    C)   145 m^2
    D)   4.5 km^2

85. Melissa is ordering fencing to enclose a square area of 5625 square feet. How many feet of fencing does she need?

    A)   75 feet
    B)   150 feet
    C)   300 feet
    D)   5,625 feet

86. Adam is painting a 4-walled shed. The shed is 5 feet wide, 4 feet deep, and 7 feet high. How much paint will Adam need?

    A)   126 ft^2
    B)   140 ft^3
    C)   63 ft^2
    D)   46 feet

87. James is building an octagonal gazebo with equal sides in his backyard. If one side is 5.5 feet wide, what is the perimeter of the entire gazebo?

    A)   22 feet
    B)   30.25 feet
    C)   44 feet
    D)   242 feet

88. A courtyard garden has flower beds in the shape of 4 equilateral triangles arranged so that their bases enclose a square space in the middle for a fountain. If the space for the fountain has an area of 1 square meter, find the total area of the flower beds and fountain space.

    A)   1.73 m^2
    B)   2.73 m^2
    C)   1.43 m^2
    D)   3 m^2

89. 2 identical circles are drawn next to each other with their sides just touching; both circles are enclosed in a rectangle whose sides are tangent to the circles. If each circle's radius is 2 inches, find the area of the rectangle.

    A)   24 cm^2
    B)   8 cm^2
    C)   32 cm^2
    D)   16 cm^2

90. A grain silo is cylinder-shaped with a height of 10 meters and a diameter of 3.2 meters. What is the surface area of the silo, including the top but not the base?

    A)   233.23 m^2
    B)   265.40 m^2
    C)   116.61 m^2
    D)   108.57 m^2

91. Find the total surface area of a box that is 12 inches long, 18 inches wide, and 6 inches high.

    A)   144 in^2
    B)   1,296 in^3
    C)   792 in^2
    D)   396 in^2

92. A developer is designing a rectangular parking lot for a new shopping center. A 20-foot-wide driving lane circles the interior, which has 6 rows of parking spaces divided by 5 driving lanes. Each row of parking spaces is 36 feet wide and 90 feet long. The driving lanes are 20 feet wide and 90 feet long. What is the perimeter of the entire parking lot?

    A)   972 feet
    B)   486 feet
    C)   812 feet
    D)   852 feet

93. A cylindrical canister is 9 inches high and has a diameter of 5 inches. What is the maximum volume this canister can hold?

    A)   176.7 in^2
    B)   45 in^2
    C)   141.4 in^2
    D)   706.9 in^2

94. If a spherical water balloon is filled with 113 milliliters of water, what is the approximate radius of the balloon?

    A)   4.0 centimeters
    B)   3.0 centimeters
    C)   3.6 centimeters
    D)   3.3 centimeters

95. A circular swimming pool has a circumference of 49 feet. What is the diameter of the pool?
- A) 15.6 feet
- B) 12.3 feet
- C) 7.8 feet
- D) 17.8 feet

96. A pizza has a diameter of 10 inches. If you cut a slice with a central angle of 40 degrees, how many inches of crust does that slice include?
- A) 31.4 inches
- B) 7.0 inches
- C) 3.5 inches
- D) 3.3 inches

97. A pizza has a diameter of 10 inches. If you cut a slice with a central angle of 40 degrees, what will be the surface area of the pizza slice?
- A) 9.2 in^2
- B) 8.7 in^2
- C) 3.5 in^2
- D) 17.4 in^2

98. Bryan drives up to a traffic circle from Elm Street. He drives 15 meters around the circle to Maple Street. If the traffic circle is a perfect circle with a radius of 10 meters, at what angle is Maple Street to Elm Street?
- A) 172°
- B) 86°
- C) 46°
- D) 14°

99. Points B and C are on a circle, and a chord is formed by line segment $\overline{BC}$. If the distance from the center of the circle to point B is 10 centimeters, and the distance from the center of the circle to line segment $\overline{BC}$ is 8 centimeters, what is the length of line segment $\overline{BC}$?
- A) 6 centimeters
- B) 4 centimeters
- C) 12 centimeters
- D) 14 centimeters

100. Liz is installing a tile backsplash. If each tile is an equilateral triangle with sides that measure 6 centimeters in length, how many tiles does she need to cover an area of 1800 square centimeters?
- A) 36 tiles
- B) 100 tiles
- C) 50 tiles
- D) 300 tiles

Mathematics Test Answer Key

1. C		47. A	
2. B		48. D	
3. A		49. C	
4. D		50. B	
5. A		51. D	
6. D		52. B	
7. C		53. B	
8. A		54. D	
9. C		55. C	
10. B		56. B	
11. C		57. A	
12. A		58. C	
13. B		59. D	
14. A		60. B	
15. D		61. C	
16. C		62. A	
17. B		63. B	
18. C		64. C	
19. A		65. A	
20. A		66. D	
21. C		67. C	
22. C		68. A	
23. D		69. C	
24. B		70. A	
25. C		71. C	
26. A		72. B	
27. D		73. D	
28. C		74. C	
29. B		75. C	
30. A		76. C	
31. D		77. A	
32. A		78. D	
33. D		79. A	
34. C		80. B	
35. A		81. D	
36. C		82. B	
37. A		83. A	
38. B		84. B	
39. A		85. C	
40. C		86. A	
41. D		87. C	
42. D		88. B	
43. B		89. C	
44. A		90. D	
45. C		91. C	
46. A		92. A	

93. A   97. B

94. B   98. B

95. A   99. C

96. C   100.   B

ParaPro Essential Test Tips DVD
from Trivium Test Prep!

Dear Customer,

Thank you for purchasing from Trivium Test Prep! We're honored to help you prepare for your ParaPro.

To show our appreciation, we're offering a **FREE *ParaPro Essential Test Tips* DVD by Trivium Test Prep**. Our DVD includes 35 test preparation strategies that will make you successful on the ParaPro. All we ask is that you email us your feedback and describe your experience with our product. Amazing, awful, or just so-so: we want to hear what you have to say!

To receive your **FREE *ParaPro Essential Test Tips* DVD**, please email us at 5star@triviumtestprep.com. Include "Free 5 Star" in the subject line and the following information in your email:

1. The title of the product you purchased.
2. Your rating from 1 – 5 (with 5 being the best).
3. Your feedback about the product, including how our materials helped you meet your goals and ways in which we can improve our products.
4. Your full name and shipping address so we can send your FREE *ParaPro Essential Test Tips* DVD.

If you have any questions or concerns please feel free to contact us directly at 5star@triviumtestprep.com.

Thank you!

- Trivium Test Prep Team

52878246R00062

Made in the USA
Middletown, DE
23 November 2017